PINK PANTIES & OTHER LIFE LESSONS

A Mindful Compendium for Adolescents

DANIELLE PARKER

THE SALTY BLOSSOM

www.thesaltyblossom.com

First paperback edition 2023

Book design by Jessica Hamm
Illustrations by Evey Parker

ISBN 979-8-9881995-0-2 (paperback)
ISBN 979-8-9881995-1-9 (ebook)

www.dwellwithdanielle.com

To Grandpa, who always knew

CONTENTS

PINK PANTIES & OTHER LIFE LESSONS

A Mindful Compendium
for Adolescents

Preface

I am not an expert. On anything. (Maybe chocolate.)

I'm telling you this up front so that you don't get halfway into the book and think to yourself, "Oh wow, she's not an expert at all," and then I'm like "Ya, you're right, I'm not that smart," and then we just stare at each other uncomfortably not knowing where to go from there.

So now we're on the same page.

Introduction
The Cave Behind the Heart

"Hidden in the heart of every creature
Exists the Self, subtler than the subtlest,
Greater than the greatest."
~Katha Upanishads

The Story

The story goes like this...

Once upon a time, we all knew exactly who we were. Then... life happened. We slowly learn to cover up our true selves. We learn that it's not ok or acceptable or safe to be our weird, silly selves. So we build layers. We hide our uniqueness, we learn not to smile or laugh, we push our emotions aside until we act like a machine version of ourselves. And then - as if that is not bad enough - we act this way for so long that we start to think this robot-self is who we actually are.

We forget who we really are.

Under these conditions, our true self becomes very small. According to the story, the true self shrinks to be the size of our thumbnail and it hides in a cave behind our hearts. Every once in a while, perfect conditions converge, we feel very comfortable, and the true self peeks out from behind the heart. We remember who we are and it feels totally natural and most excellent. In the next moment, however, we pull back and it disappears once more.

It is said that our job in this life is very simple:
REMEMBER WHO YOU ARE

You Forgot, Didn't You?

I bet you two bars of ultra deluxe artisanal chocolate from a tiny shop in Taos, New Mexico, that this has already happened to you. Think about it. When we're young, we let our Crazy Flag fly wildly. My son wore undies and a superman cape for at least a year. My daughter told awful - AWFUL - knock knock jokes while laughing hysterically. They did that without a second thought about what people might think or say. The next time you're in public, notice how often little kids laugh. They are ridiculous. For real. It's out of control. They skip, they jump over stones, they chase bubbles with pure joy.

And then...

And then we learn that we should care about what other people think or say about us. We learn that what others say can hurt us and that people won't take us seriously if we are joyful or silly. We learn that the worst feeling in the world is to not belong. So we take evasive action. Instead of chasing bubbles, we sneer at them and pretend we don't care. We work really hard to stop smiling. In fact, we smother most emotions because it doesn't feel safe to express them. Layer upon layer, we cover up our true bubble-loving selves. That true self shrinks down and moves into the cave behind our hearts, just waiting for the opportunity to shine once again.

An Example

I love to surf. I paddle surf, standing on the board and using a paddle to sweep me into the next wave. I am a clumsy surfer, wiping out on waves more often than I ride them. I'm also scared of surfing. Every time I go out, I have to move past the breakers and paddle around for 20 minutes or so until I muster the nerve to actually attempt to surf.

So weird.

Eventually, I will see a wave coming. Paddle paddle paddle! I either don't catch the wave at all or I catch it, I get suddenly nervous, and I nosedive off the front. This is my pattern.

Sometimes, accidentally, I catch a wave. I won't really be paying attention or concentrating. A wave is suddenly upon me and I randomly paddle a bit. In the first moment when I realize I am riding a wave, I think, "Oh that was easy. Why don't I just do that every time?"

And then the magic happens.

Everything falls away. There are no distractions. There are no thoughts in my head. There is no sense of time. Am I even breathing? It is just me and the wave. Everything is easy, clear. Pure joy.

The ride only lasts a handful of seconds. I am off my board, swirling in the water, and all I want is to find that feeling again. So, out I paddle, struggling through oncoming waves, questioning my ability, succumbing to and then facing my fear. Just so I can experience a few seconds of unfiltered, supreme excellence.

This is my true self. Surfing creates the situation for it to peek out from behind my heart. There is no thinking, no ego. It is simply me.

We all have these moments although the events that uncover them are different from person to person. It happens when a joyful calm washes over you and the thoughts cease.

There is no thinking, just existing.

The more aware we are of these moments, the more often we can capture them. The more we capture them, the more they will happen and the longer they will last. The longer they last, the more we start to remember.

Layer by layer, we uncover the true self hiding in the caves behind our hearts.

This story of the cave and the true self appears in the Upanishads. These are ancient texts written between 800-200 B.C. The fact that they focus on the discovery of the Self is proof that this is an issue that transcends time. People have been wondering about this for centuries. From the Kena Upanishad, "There is only one way to know the Self, And that is to realize him yourself."

This is a process, a journey, and as Lao Tzu reminds us, "The journey of a thousand miles begins with one step."

May this book guide you there.

(And if not, may it be a useful coaster for your soda or perhaps you could wedge it under the leg of a wobbly table.)

Part I

In which I spend several chapters convincing you that you should read this book.

1

The Pink Panty Incident

A Pink Story

I don't like the color pink. It's soft and gentle and I am neither of those things. I am tough and strong and super fast. That's what I was thinking that morning in third grade when my life was about to change forever.

My mom loves pink. Pink everything. Socks, hair bands, a long swirly skirt that she wears everywhere. With ruffles. I am so not ruffly and I am definitely not pink.

You can imagine my dismay when I opened the drawer to get dressed that morning – the most important morning of the year – and the only pair of underwear left is that one pair of pink panties. Pale pink. Pastel pink. The worst kind...

Today is a day to impress. This is the one day of the school year when people nod their heads in approval as I speed by. Today is Field Day. We will spend the day outside on the field engaging in a variety of games and races. I am tiny, the smallest student in the class. Maybe that's why it surprises everyone when I win most of the races.

I am lightning fast, streaking ahead in the 100 yard dash! I am strong, beating all the boys in the class! I am coordinated, winning the three legged race no matter who they partner me beside! Don't get me started on the sack race. I am a warrior!

A warrior wearing pale pink panties.

It's ok, I tell myself, no one will know.

The day is indeed glorious. I revel in the attention of being unexpectedly good at something. One of my many boyfriends, Bradley, is by my side, only a little jealous of my success. As the day winds down, we come to the final event.

It is a relay race. It will involve our entire team. Whoever wins this, wins Field Day. The team quickly decides that I will go last, since I am Super Amazing.

The race begins!

The sun is shining; the adrenaline is pumping; the noise is deafening. When it's my turn, I don't hesitate. I put on the team uniform, an overly large pair of shorts and shirt and I'm off! I am neck-in-neck with the other team's last player as well. We speed through the obstacles. Bounce the ball three times, make a basket, scooter back to the starting line.

I'm there! I won! I tear off my team uniform and prepare to walk over triumphantly to my team.

It takes me a minute to realize something is wrong. It's way too quiet. Why isn't the team screaming for me? Why are there a zillion eyeballs staring at me? Why do their faces look completely empty?

My best friend Kate runs to my side and pulls on my arm. I look down.

Pale.

Pink.

Panties.

In my hurry to pull off the team uniform, I pulled off my regular shorts as well. I am standing in front of the entire 3rd grade class wearing only a shirt and my pink panties.

Well.

There is really only one thing to do.

Run away.

I pull up my pants, grab Kate, and run away into the neighboring field. I cry and cry and cry. WHY?! Why did I have to wear the pink panties today?

I am filled with embarrassment and shame. I am not a pink panty person! Today was supposed to be the day of strength and courage and now it is just filled with failure. Can't they see that this is not really who I am??

Finally, a teacher shows up and takes control. The damage has been done though. As we are paraded back to class, I can see the pitying eyes of my classmates. I am no longer strong or fast. I am now the sad girl in pink panties.

Sometimes Things Are Yucky

Our lives are filled with Pink Panty Incidents. These moments when it feels like we are watching pieces of our lives fall apart. Or even worse: we are watching other people watch us as our lives fall apart. In those moments, it feels to me as if I am standing completely still and the world is swirling around me. When the swirling stops, I know that nothing will be the same again.

I often think about my life as Before the incident and After the incident. Before this happened, I was a super popular, totally awesome 3rd grader. I had at least 5 boyfriends who would chase me during recess. I mean, does life get any better than that? (Well, yeah, it totally does but not for 3rd grade me.) I was confident and tough. Life was good. After the incident, no one in class would talk to me. My boyfriends all dumped me and started calling me "Medusa". I became tough in a different way. People did forget the incident eventually, but not before I pulled away from everyone and became the girl who tries to hide and not draw attention to herself. (Sad face)

There's this really cool lady named Deidre Blomfield-Brown. She went through the first part of her life just as you and I probably are: school, friends, hobbies, relationships, etc. Then, in her 30s, her second marriage fell apart. This was a horrible, very bad, life-shattering event for her. It was her Pink Panty Incident. Soon after, she became a Buddhist nun and was renamed Pema Chodron. Having survived a truly difficult situation, she turned her efforts into helping others do the same. She has written many books to help people deal with life's difficulties.

Pema refers to these Pink Panty Incidents as those moments in which "things fall apart." In those moments, our survival instincts kick in. We immediately want to do whatever it takes to move away from the source of pain. For many of us, this is running away. We think that something is wrong and we need to escape. For me in 3rd grade, I literally ran away from everyone; unfortunately, to no avail. (Cue dramatic music - preferably violin.)

This incident is not the only time in my life when I really wanted to run away. In fact, I have a picture saved on my phone. It's a picture of a cave. Beautiful cave. It has twinkle lights inside as well as a pool. This is the cave I am going to run away to the next time things fall apart. Whenever I start feeling that way, I pull up the picture and fantasize about how great it would be to live in this cave, all alone, where life can't surprise me and no one can ever hurt me again. It's going to be glorious. You're not invited.

I still haven't ventured to that cave though. Perhaps I am smarter than I was in 3rd grade. (It's possible.) Either that or I'm lazy. (It's possible.)

Here's the thing:

There was this guy named Siddhartha Guatama, though you probably know him better as the Buddha. (Kind of a big deal.) He created a philosophy that attempted to explain life in all of its glory and yuckiness. The first thing he says about Life is that Pink Panty Incidents are inevitable. They are going to happen throughout our lives, no matter what we do. It doesn't matter how prepared we are, how smart we are, how popular we are. NO MATTER WHAT, yucky events are going to happen. Regardless of who you are or how many 3rd grade boyfriends you have, sometimes life sucks.

Not only that, but get this: He also says that there is nothing wrong with Pink Panty Incidents. This is kind of a mind-blowing idea. Most people in our lives, from parents to teachers to your favorite barista, tell us to do everything we can to AVOID unfortunate situations.

"Always be prepared."

"Prepare for the worst."

"Think, Dana, think!" (Oh wait, that might have just been my mom.)

The Buddha, on the other hand, said that we really can't do anything to avoid Pink Panty Incidents. Regardless of what we do, they are going to happen. It doesn't matter how prepared we are, they are going to happen. Despite hiding in a cave and avoiding all possible situations, they are going to happen. They are inevitable. Sooooooo...if they are going to happen no matter what, then maybe they aren't the Worst Possible Thing. Maybe they are just a part of life. We should, in fact, expect them.

Pink Panty Incidents are not an anomaly (big word meaning a crazy & ridiculous event). Perhaps, Pink Panty Incidents are normal. There's nothing wrong with them. They don't feel good, for sure, but I will survive. I don't have to run away. Even if I run away, I will still suffer. (Just ask 3rd grade me.)

That's why I've never visited that cave. I'd probably sprain my ankle going down the intricately carved stone stairs or electrocute myself on the twinkle lights. The escape is no escape at all.

When you no longer have to run away, things become amazingly easier. But scary. Not running away is really scary because that means you have to face things, whether that is a bad decision, a failed relationship, or wearing pink panties in front of the entire class.

Ok. So this changes everything. We don't need to be scared of whether a Pink Panty Incident is going to happen or not. It's totally going to happen. I no longer need to be scared about that.

Problem solved.

Kind of.

Well, not really.

Umm...

WHAT AM I SUPPOSED TO DO WHEN SOMETHING LIKE THIS HAPPENS?

What Do We Do???

Right. Right right right riggghhhhht. We don't need to worry about yuckiness happening but I guess we still need to overthink how we are supposed to survive them when they do happen. How do we channel our inner Buddha so that Pink Panty Incidents are, like, no big deal?

I guess we have some work to do. Let's write out some guidelines as we go to keep ourselves organized.

LIFE LESSON #1: Never wear pink panties.

Let me try again.

LIFE LESSON #1: Sometimes, life sucks.

Chapter Summary

- We often dread or are scared of embarrassing, cringe-worthy events happening.
- The Buddha says, don't worry. They will totally happen.
- In fact, we can expect that our lives will be filled with an assortment of uncomfortable situations.
- Sweet relief: We no longer need to worry about it because now we know they will indeed happen.
- What do we do about them? Keep reading.

To-Do List

Think about the supremely awful, melt-into-the-floorboards moments of your life so far. Pretend you are a movie producer making a short film about this event.

Choose one of the following activities to complete:

- Draw a movie poster that portrays the film.
- Create a comic strip version of the story for the producer to read.
- Write the script of this film.
- Craft a letter from future you written to past you about this event. What would you want past you to know? (This letter will be read dramatically at the end of the film.)

When Life Events Are Not Ok

This chapter is explaining how sometimes life sucks. (Yup, so true.) Let's take a moment and pause to make sure we are all on the same page.

Pink Panty Incidents are events that are annoying, embarrassing, and cringe-worthy. Here are a few examples (apart from the obvious pink panties of my past):

- When you lay your head down at the end of class and all of your classmates think you are asleep so they start talking about you not knowing that you can hear everything they are saying.
- Playing around next to your dad's shoe shine machine but your hair gets too close to it. It gets tangled and you have to cut your hair out of it.
- When you make a very important presentation to your teachers but they are using a new online format and they don't realize that, while you are presenting, you can read all of the negative comments they are making about you.

All of those things have happened to me. I am not even kidding.

Pink Panty Incidents are unfortunate and they feel yucky BUT they do not create lasting harm. Pink Panty Incidents do NOT refer to situations in which you are emotionally or physically abused by another person. These types of situations are never acceptable and they are not something that you should put up with as "just part of life."

Sometimes it is hard to ask for help. If you find yourself in an unacceptable situation, find a friend or a trusted adult to confide in. Together, you can work to find the help required to change your situation.

2

Olive Green Boots

An Unfortunate Story (Or Fortunate?)

Once upon a time, there was a farmer who lived with his wife and son. They raised horses and then sold them to the community as a way of life. The family members were hard workers and compassionate tenders of their horses. They did well for themselves.

They were very excited because they had put much effort into preparing a horse and they were ready to sell it for such a profit that it would get them through the cold, winter months. The night before the transaction, a huge storm hit the area. There was much precipitation but it was the wind that did real damage. The wind blew down all of their fences and their prized horse ran away in terror.

When they woke up the next morning and saw that they had no horses, the wife exclaimed, "How unfortunate that this would have happened!" The neighbors came over and sympathized with her.

The farmer, however, stood still, looked around, and said, "Fortunate or unfortunate? We just don't know. We'll have to wait and see."

A week later, the family was sitting at the table eating breakfast. As they looked out the window, they saw an entire herd of horses running towards the farm. It turns out that their prized horse did run away, but he had returned and had brought several other horses with him. The family would be able to work with these horses to create additional income for their farm.

The wife was ecstatic with joy. "Look what has happened! How fortunate!"

The farmer, however, stood still, looked around, and said, "Fortunate or unfortunate? We just don't know. We'll have to wait and see."

One of the new horses was a young stallion. The farmer gave the son permission to train this horse all by himself. The son was excited as this would be the first time he was trusted to take on this task. One day during training, the stallion bucked wildly and threw the son off his back.

The son broke every bone in his body.

The neighbors came over to console the wife. "How unfortunate!" they all said.

The farmer, however, stood still, looked around, and said, "Fortunate or unfortunate? We just don't know. We'll have to wait and see."

The son slowly began to heal though he was confined to his bed. During this time, the kingdom was plunged into war and the king sent his men through the countryside to round up any young, able-bodied men to fight in the war.

The king's men removed many sons from neighboring families. When they came to the farmer's house, however, they saw that the son could hardly move. The son would be of no help in a war, so the king's men left without him.

The wife was immensely relieved not to lose her son to a war. The neighbors all came over, grief-stricken at losing their sons. As they consoled each other, they exclaimed, "How fortunate that your son was not taken!"

As we know, however, the farmer stood still, looked around, and said, "Fortunate or unfortunate? We just don't know. We'll have to wait and see."

A year passed and the son healed completely. He was back to his normal activities with much enthusiasm. Meanwhile, the king had lost so many men in the war that he did not have enough workmen to attend to his castle. He sent his men out through the countryside once again to find any men that could come work at the castle. They came upon the farmer's son and told him that he was required to leave his house and move to the castle to be a groundskeeper immediately.

The wife was heartbroken. She said goodbye to her son and fell into a deep depression. The neighbors came over to support her.

"How unfortunate," they whispered, "that this should happen."

The farmer, not surprisingly, stood still, looked around, and said, "Fortunate or unfortunate? We just don't know. We'll have to wait and see."

The son was a dedicated and joyful worker who had a talent for his new job. It should be mentioned that the king had a beautiful and intelligent daughter and it may come as no surprise that she fell in love with the son.

The following spring, the farmer and his wife received a message telling them of the marriage of the princess to their son. The farmer and his wife were not only invited to the wedding but were also invited to come and live at the castle, where they would be taken care of, for the rest of their lives.

The wife threw a party and invited all of the neighbors. There was much celebration and happiness shared throughout the night.

"How fortunate that this would happen to you!" Everyone exclaimed.

As for the farmer... Well he stood still, looked around, and said, "Fortunate or unfortunate? We just don't know. We'll have to wait and see."

This is the end of the story although I think we all know that the story never truly ends. This event was followed by another event and another and another and another. Some were fortunate and some unfortunate...or were they?

Is it possible that there is no such thing as fortunate and unfortunate? Is it possible that there are simply events, one that leads to another, and it is not possible to determine what is actually fortunate or unfortunate?

We'll come back to that.

Grasping & Avoiding

STOP. Right there. Don't read another word.

Well, ok, read these words.

And a few more.

Let me try again: Read these words in consecutive order but don't skip ahead.

Before we continue, I need you to grab a sheet of scrap paper and something to write with. If you are truly desperate, go ahead and write in the margin of this book. (Unless it's a library book as librarians are oddly intense about that sort of thing.)

On your scrap paper, think about 3 times you were unhappy. Jot down why you were unhappy. I don't need the whole story. Just the end result. Example: I was unhappy because I really wanted a pair of olive green boots but they did not have my size.

Go ahead. Write down your three things.

I'll wait.

.

.

.

.

.

Got it? Good.

We learned in the last chapter that sometimes life sucks. Let's talk about why.

It boils down to one very simple thing: Everybody wants to be happy.

There is definitely nothing wrong with this. The 14th Dalai Lama has even stated, "The purpose of life is to be happy."

So where are we going wrong???

Ah, little cricket, patience. All shall be revealed in the next sentence:

We think the source of happiness is external to ourselves. We think that something out there in the world is going to bring us happiness.

To clarify, we will work incredibly hard to be happy. The problem is that the things we believe will bring us happiness are not actual sources of happiness.

Let's talk about boots. (I love boots.) When I was growing up, beginning at about the time I became an adolescent, my grandparents started giving me money for Christmas. Every year, I would buy a new pair of boots. (I love boots.) Every single year, I would pine for a pair of boots and I would tell myself, "This is the last pair of boots you will ever need to buy. Look at how beautiful and perfect they are. Once you own these boots, you will be so happy and never want for boots again." Guess what? I would indeed buy the boots and feel wonderfully fulfilled and happy. Then...a few months later, I would start daydreaming about boots again. (I love boots.)

The boots did indeed bring me happiness, but not the kind that lasts. This is true of many of our wants, right? Think about it. Have you ever wanted something so very badly and you told yourself something along the lines of, "If I could just _____, then I would be happy." You can fill in the blank with lots of different things. Here are a few examples:

If I had a billion dollars...

If I could find true love...

If I could get a car...

If I could never go to school again...

If I could write an amazing book about mindfulness and then become famous and then talk to Oprah who would solve all of my life's problems and then have enough money that I would always have fancy artisanal chocolate in my pocket...

Unfortunately, none of those things tend to bring lasting happiness. After the amazingness of my new boots wear off, I just want a different pair. The moment you do super amazing in algebra class, you have to begin geometry and you're back to feeling unhappy and unintelligent.

If the purpose of life is indeed to be happy, how do we do this? Well, we're not actually ready to answer that question yet. First, let's talk about why we are unhappy.

Grasping and Avoiding. That's why.

Grasping and avoiding are the two sources of unhappiness. Remember that all of us really, truly, extraordinarily want nothing more than to be supremely happy. There are two methods that we use to do this.

Grasping means that we try to hold tightly - too tightly! - onto things that we think will bring us happiness. Olive green boots. True love. New car. Oprah Winfrey. We tell ourselves that we will be happy if only, if only, we have that special something. We convince ourselves of this so completely that sometimes it is hard to think about anything else. All thoughts are consumed about where to buy the boots online, what size I should order, how long it will take to receive them in the mail, how intensely amazing I will look when I am wearing them. This is grasping and it does not feel good.

Think about it. Does it feel good to want something so completely and not to have it? This is a form of unhappiness. We will do whatever we can to obtain that thing, whatever it is, so that we can stop feeling so horribly. Obtaining that item does not actually bring happiness, it simply takes away the yucky feeling of grasping for it!

Many of us grasp towards physical objects and money but it can happen with emotions too. Suppose you are a very lonely person. You always feel like you stick out in a crowd. You are nervous to speak to new people and often feel overlooked. What you want more than anything is to feel loved and to belong. Wild situations transpire and you find yourself in a relationship with an attentive, loving partner. Her friends and family all accept you as an amazing addition to their groups. You have never been happier.

Uh oh.

This is what you have wanted your whole life. You can't go back to how things used to be. What would you do if she ever dumped you??? Above all else, that CANNOT happen.

So you grasp tighter to the relationship. You need this relationship more than anything in the world. You give her so much attention so that she won't feel neglected. You smother her with expressions of your love. You spend every available moment with her. You make sure she never remembers what it's like to be without you.

You can imagine that this story does not end well. You are no longer acting like yourself but rather a crazed version of yourself. By grasping so very tightly to her, you end up pushing her away. She dumps you and you are left to wonder how this could have possibly happened.

Imagine what it would feel like to grasp so tightly to someone out of fear of losing them. Grasping does not feel good. We grasp in an effort to bring happiness but the end result is an unfulfilling, needy feeling. We have made ourselves unhappy.

Now, let's shift to avoiding. In our search for happiness, the one thing we know for sure is that there are certain things that make us miserable: getting cavities filled, feeling alone, being rejected by others, the list goes on. When we are not trying to obtain items (grasping), we spend our time avoiding those things that we are scared will make us unhappy.

It sounds brilliant, right? I know that being judged by others makes me feel vulnerable and bad about myself. So, in order to not feel this unhappiness, I work really hard to conform to whatever all the other students in my class are doing. Even though I don't agree with what they are wearing or doing or saying, I just go along with it because that way they think I am one of them and they won't judge me. Super easy. All I have to do is forget who I really am, push down my personal opinions, and look the other way when they do or say something mean or inappropriate about others.

Oh wait...

That doesn't sound like happiness. In fact, it sounds like the worst. THE WORST.

In my attempt to avoid the thing that makes me unhappy, I unintentionally made myself unhappier than I would have been had I faced things head on.

How about another example? My son is scared of getting shots. Crazy scared. Like, so scared that I wonder how he is possibly my son.

He tries to avoid shots at all costs because he knows they make him unhappy. Every time he gets a shot, afterwards he admits that it wasn't actually that bad. Then the next opportunity arrives and he loses his mind again.

A few years ago, at his annual doctor's appointment, the doctor knew he was scared of shots and she offered him the opportunity to get his immunization shots right then or to wait one year until his next appointment. Despite my pleas that he get it out of the way and the reminders that it's not really that bad, he chose to avoid the situation and put it off for another year.

Guess how that year went? Not well, people. It did not go well.

At least once every week, my son would bring up the upcoming shots. He would count down how much time was remaining and how he sure was glad it wasn't happening today. As the appointment drew closer, his panic grew immensely larger. He started having intense anxiety about it. He would start crying and hyperventilating when we tried to talk about it.

In his attempt to avoid the situation, he made himself miserable. He went from having a dislike to having a phobia. He shifted from having a few moments of discomfort to having panic attacks.

May we all learn from his foible: Avoiding unhappiness will produce larger levels of unhappiness.

Good Versus Bad

It would appear that our happiness-seeking brains are working unconsciously in ways that undermine that happiness. Not cool, brain. Here's a question: How do our brains decide which things to grasp onto and which things to avoid?

Mmm-hmm. Excellent question. One that will bring us full circle to revisit the farmer, his wife, and their son. In order to either grasp or avoid, we have to first label things as being either "good" or "bad". We are, in fact, making a list and we're checking it twice.

Good	Bad
• New olive green boots	• Getting shots
• Finding love	• Dentist appointments

Our brains like to label things. Once we label things, we feel more organized. It helps us to make sense of the world around us.

BUT.

But but but.

This leads to a cycle. We label something as good. We start to grasp for that thing. We grasp so tightly that we then feel unhappy. On the other hand, we label something as bad. We avoid that thing in order to be happy but in that process we become even more unhappy.

Linking this back to the farmer and his wife, think about how each of them reacted to the various situations they went through. Through the course of that story, the wife was on an emotional roller coaster. Every time she labeled something as unfortunate, she suffered. Every time she labeled something as fortunate, she was flying high, only to sink down when the next unfortunate event occurred.

The farmer, on the other hand, did not label things as good/bad, fortunate/unfortunate. He stood back, took in the situations, reacted in any way that was necessary, but did not suffer.

Let's think about it. When the horse ran away, the wife decided this was unfortunate. Was it? If the horse had not run away, then he would not have returned with an entire herd of horses. So was this actually unfortunate?

Similarly, when the horses returned, the wife decided this was fortunate. Again I ask, was it? If the horses had not returned, then the son would not have been given a horse to train and he would never have broken every bone in his body. Was this really fortunate?

We can follow the events of this story in a similar way. For every fortunate or unfortunate incident, ask yourself, "But was it?"

Our lives are very similar. One event leads to another, which leads to another, which leads to another, and another, and another, and you get what I'm saying. Events are only fortunate or unfortunate in the instant that they happen. Beyond that, they lead to another event and another. There is, in fact, no way to tell if events are actually fortunate or unfortunate. If we removed just one event from your timeline, the course of your life would completely change!

The question this leaves us with: Is it actually helpful for our brains to label things as good or bad? I would say no. But then again, I would say a lot of things, such as I need a new pair of boots. Really, this is a question for you to ponder.

In Act II, Scene 2, of William Shakespeare's "Hamlet", Hamlet states, "There is nothing either good or bad, but thinking makes it so." Indeed Hamlet appears to be very wise in this statement. Events are just events. It is our brain's interpretation of the events that make them fortunate or unfortunate.

The solution: curiosity. (It killed the cat but we should be ok.)

If we decide to stop labeling things but act instead with curiosity, as the farmer did, then we don't have to partake in the Brain's Wild Ride of emotions. We won't shut down every time something "bad" happens. We won't grasp and avoid those good and bad things. We won't, in summary, increase our unhappiness.

Danielle Tells a Story

I first heard the story of the farmer when I was going through yoga teacher training. My teacher told us the story, she explained the moral of the story, and then she told us this:

Instead of saying something is good or bad, simply say that it is interesting.

"Well, isn't that interesting."

I thought, uh yeah, ok, as if that would work. I am truly talented at labeling things. One little sentence isn't going to change all of that.

So, like the annoying student I was, I started to say the phrase in a very sarcastic, kind-of-making-fun-of-her way. (I sincerely hope you are better students than I have been in the past.)

For example, I would stub my toe, scream in pain, and then in a fake philosophical tone, I would state, "Well, isn't that interesting."

I would get all red lights while driving to an appointment and arrive too late. I would return to my car, adopt a most brilliant English accent, and exclaim, "Well, isn't that interesting!"

I would get an extraordinarily fabulous present in the mail from a friend and, after jumping up and down in joy, I would put my hands on my hips and ask my husband, "Well now, isn't that interesting?"

Unfortunately (or fortunately), I have to admit that my teacher was correct. Although I started doing this from a critical space, it accidentally became a habit. Over time, I lost my contempt for the practice. I don't know how it happened because I definitely wasn't trying to do that (as you can see), but I now say this phrase all the time. Quite sincerely.

I don't exclaim it. I don't yell or even direct it towards anyone. It's totally low key. Something will happen, and instead of judging it, I will say to myself or even mumble out loud, "Huh. Isn't that interesting?".

It is not good or bad. It is just interesting.

I don't plunge up and down uncomfortably on the emotional roller coaster depending on what I determine to be good or bad. (Well, I definitely still do that but not as much as I used to.) I observe. Instead of judging myself and others, I find things completely, wonderfully interesting. Captivating. I can't wait to see what happens next.

As you remove some of the sources of your unhappiness, guess what floats to the top all on its own: happiness (contentment, joy...choose the word that feels best).

~~LIFE LESSON #2 - Buy new boots.~~
Almost. One more try.
LIFE LESSON #2 - Well, isn't that interesting.

Chapter Summary

- When we label something as being "good", we often grasp towards it so tightly that we become unhappy.
- When we label something as being "bad", we often avoid it so intensely that we become unhappy.
- If we stop labeling things but become curious instead, we remove these sources of unhappiness.
- As we remove unhappiness, it turns out that happiness is right there waiting for us.

To-Do List

- Look at your list of unhappy events that you wrote down earlier while reading this chapter. Can you distinguish whether they are the result of grasping or avoiding?
- Create your own version of the Fortunate or Unfortunate story. Use modern day events and people.
  - Draw a comic showing the story.
  - Write it out as a short story.
  - Create a children's book out of the story.
  - Write a skit and act it out.

3

I Think Therefore I Eat Chocolate

Don't Go to Sea with Me

When I was in college, instead of doing a study abroad semester, I chose to do something called SEA semester. Instead of going to a foreign country for a few months, I went to the ocean. My classmates and I spent 6 weeks on land learning everything we would need to know to survive at sea: navigation, oceanography, maritime studies, and some other stuff I've clearly forgotten. Then, we went to sea and applied those skills. We sailed in a 134-foot brigantine schooner (fancy name for big sailboat). We departed from Woods Hole, MA, traveled down through the Atlantic Ocean and then throughout the Caribbean, eventually landing in Antigua six weeks later. While sailing, we were not allowed to use technology. We had a compass to steer the ship but we were not allowed GPS. We had to navigate by the position of the stars, just like the good ol' days.

What an adventure! I thought. This is going to be the best experience of my life! I might love it so much that I'll never go back to land!

The first day was fun.

The second day was a little tiring.

On the third day, nauseous.

But the fourth day? On the fourth day, reality hit.

A combination of weather from Hurricane Michael and hitting the Gulf Stream resulted in high seas with 15 foot swells. The ship was casting back and forth so intensely that anyone who was on deck had to wear a harness that was attached via rope to the ship just in case we were swept overboard. When the ship would sway to one side, that side of the ship was almost parallel to the water.

While on the sailing vessel, my classmates and I were assigned to groups. We worked with our groups for the entire journey, rotating through 5 different possible shifts (called watches) per day: two 6-hour day watches and three 4-hour night watches.

Guess who had night watch during the 15 foot seas?

Guess who was asked to steer the ship at night during the 15 foot seas?

Allow me to paint a picture. The ship was rolling from side to side and it was difficult to stand in one place. As waves crashed, saltwater sprayed my face forcing me to squint in order to see. My left contact fell out so I had only one "working" eye. Night in the open ocean is DARK, people. There was minimal lighting on deck, making it even harder to see anything around me, least of all the compass.

Regardless of these conditions, there I stood at the helm. I was holding onto the wheel for dear life, partly to help keep myself planted in one place and partly because if I took a hand off the wheel it would start spinning and the ship would careen in a different direction. There was a compass located a few feet in front of the helm. The first mate was overseeing me and he gave me a compass heading.

"Just keep the ship heading in this direction. That's all you need to do."

All I need to do...eye roll.

With each 15 foot swell, the ship would shift direction and it was my job to hold tight to the helm and redirect it back on course. Simultaneously, with each 15 foot swell, saltwater stung my eyes making it nearly impossible to see the compass in front of me. The helm, I might mention, was as tall as me and the power of the waves was incredibly strong. It was more like the wheel was moving me around instead of the opposite.

"Watch the compass! Come on now - just move the wheel!"

In the calm between waves, I would focus on the compass and use all of my tiny muscle strength to pull the wheel into the correct heading. Then the next wave would come and we would be off course again.

Over and over and over again.

"What's your heading?! Correct course. Now!"

It was a long night.

<Pause for dramatic effect. And because just thinking about it makes me feel exhausted.>

Every person would have reacted differently to that experience. Were I to have this experience now, I would react differently than I did when I was 20. At that particular point in my life, this is how I reacted:

Every time a wave knocked the ship off course, I felt like I was doing something wrong. Every time the first mate yelled at me, I thought he was mad at me for totally messing it up. I was scared; I couldn't see; I kept getting soaked with saltwater; the ship looked (to me) like it was about to capsize.

Overall, I thought: I CAN'T DO THIS!

After that incredibly challenging night, I was scared to steer the ship. For the rest of the journey, I would try everything I could to escape having that job. I would volunteer for other jobs immediately. I would shrink into the background when they asked who wanted to steer. The only time I would do it was when the first mate told me I had no choice.

Every time I stood at the helm for the rest of those 6 weeks, I was terrified. There was a voice in my head telling me that I couldn't do this. You're going to mess it up. You're going to get us lost at sea. You're not strong enough, smart enough, brave enough to do this. Every time, I chose to believe that voice.

Now, as a rational person, you are probably reading this thinking, "Wow, she's overreacting." I grant that you're probably right.

Let's take another look at those events. As a rational person, you would probably see it differently than 20-year-old me. You would probably notice that the weather was super crazy, creating high seas. Not my fault. It was the first few days out at sea and I had never steered a 134 foot ship before. Not my fault. As the waves arrived, the physics of the situation dictated that the ship would be thrown off course. Not my fault. In general, when saltwater is splashed in your face, it creates a burning sensation in the eyes that forces you to squeeze your eyes shut. It can then take a moment to readjust to looking around you. Not my fault.

In fact, when we really look at it, there was no aspect of that situation that was my fault. I followed every direction given to me. I continued to stand at the helm even after I was thrown around again and again. I did not get us lost at sea. Every person on the ship survived the night. If we are very honest, my dedication and determination in the face of a new and scary situation is commendable. I did, in fact, act admirably.

In light of all of these very obvious facts, why did I walk away from that situation feeling like a terrible person who was then scared to stand at the helm forevermore?

To answer that question, we need to take a walk in the forest.

Let's Go for a Walk

Let's head into the forest. Walk with me. Here we go, down the path, right into the forest. Take a look around. Tall trees, each one with unique bark, like tree fingerprints. The trees are thick in our forest. They stand close together with branches interwoven.

I don't like the heat, so let's make this imaginary journey a crisp, fall day. Gaze upwards - see the sunlight silhouetting the brittle many-colored leaves.

And we're walking, we're walking...

Listen to the crunch of the brittle leaves under your feet. Can you smell them? Oh man, I love that smell. How about that tingle on your cheeks from the chilly air? The best.

Where are we going, by the way?

As I look around, I see that we are on a path that is cutting through the trees. It is a wide and easy path. You can tell it has been traveled often. It would be very easy to stay on this path and enjoy the walk.

But really, when I think about it, we can walk anywhere, right? I don't HAVE to stay on the path. I could choose to veer off the path and walk straight into the scraggly underbrush of the forest.

What do we think about that option?

Pro: It would be more of an adventure. We might see some cool things that we wouldn't see from the path.

Con: It would be really hard to make a new path through the trees. The trees are close together and all of those branches are literally everywhere. We would probably get tangled up. Would we get lost? Maybe it would be scary in there. What even lives in this forest?!

Which path do you choose?

There Are So Many Paths

Our brains are composed of special brain cells, called neurons. It is estimated that there are between 80-100 billion neurons in the brain. BILLION. Seems like a lot.

The neurons are what create the thoughts we have. Every time neurons connect to each other, they share information and we have some sort of thought. So, when different neurons connect, we have different thoughts. The number of thoughts we can have is only limited by the number of connections available in the brain. Since each neuron can connect to many other neurons, there are a possible 100 trillion different connections. TRILLION. Definitely a lot.

This means that, technically, there could be 100 trillion different thoughts that I could have at any one moment.

Huh.

Why is it, then, that I am constantly thinking about chocolate? Literally. Right now, I am thinking about the huge bag of chocolate chips in the pantry and how I could stop typing and just go over and grab a handful.

Do you know how many times a day I think about chocolate? Probably a trillion.

If there are so many different thoughts I could be having, why are they all about chocolate? Why can't I start thinking about broccoli? That would be way healthier for me.

Ugh. I just thought about broccoli. Not cool.

It turns out, our brains and our thought patterns are very similar to the forest we walked through a few minutes ago. The path that was already present in the forest was so very easy to walk on. We could walk and not even think about it. We wouldn't even need to focus on where we were going. We would just go.

To create a new path, however, would be crazy hard. We would need to focus intensely on what we were doing. Each step would have been difficult. I would be exhausted and need lots of chocolate to keep going. The easiest part would have been giving up and heading back to the smooth path.

Let's imagine, just for a sec, that we did forge a new path. What if we took that new path every time we walked in the forest? On each walk, we could choose this new path. At first, it would be tricky and annoying. Over time, though, it would start to become easier to travel. Eventually, we would be able to walk on it without effort. Meanwhile, if we totally ignored the other path, over time, the trees would slowly overtake it. That initially smooth path, if ignored, would disappear.

This same concept is true in our brains. Each thought we have is a specific neural pathway. When we have the same thought over and over again, that pathway becomes stronger and stronger. The thought will start happening even when we don't realize it. It could start running in the background of our minds while we are sitting doing our algebra homework. <Chocolate is yummy. I want chocolate.> When our parents are talking to us at dinner, we could simultaneously be having this thought. <Chocolate would be yummier than this broccoli.> When we take a break from chores, we would immediately think this thought. <Grab some yummy chocolate from the pantry.>

This thought pathway is the smooth, easy-to-travel path in the forest. No effort. It just happens.

Why don't I think about how yummy broccoli is? That would be a completely new thought for me. I have never in my life had that thought. Connecting those neurons in order to have that thought would take a lot of effort. It would be like leaving the path and striking out into the trees in the forest. Uncomfortable. Challenging. Maybe even exhausting. (Quick - bring some chocolate.)

Therefore, as a human who follows the path of least resistance, I unconsciously continue to have the easy thought. The natural thought. The thought that does not take any effort. Regardless of whether or not that thought has positive or negative effects on me.

With that, I think we're ready to head back to sea.

Out on the Atlantic Ocean, in the 134 foot sailing vessel, I am beating myself up for being so incredibly terrible at steering. Even though all of the facts indicate that there is nothing in that situation about which I should feel poorly.

Why was I immune to logic? Why did I choose to ignore all practical thought so that I could feel like I was a person of no worth?

I thought all those things about myself because, at that time in my life, that was the largest, smoothest path in my neural forest. Without effort, the easiest path for my neurons to make were those that told me I was not good enough. Despite the 100 trillion other options out there for me to think, my mind chose to focus on that path.

Sense of Thought

We make order out of our lives through the input from our senses. Out at sea in the middle of the night, I could feel the wind on my body. This informed me that there was a storm. I could see 15 foot seas. This informed me that I needed to be careful as I walked on deck. I could taste the saltwater in my mouth. This informed me that it was the water from the ocean waves that was hitting my face repeatedly. All of our senses relay information to our brains by which we understand what is happening around us.

Notice something interesting about this. I see 15 foot seas but I am not 15 foot seas. That's simply something I can see with my eyes. I feel saltwater on my face but I am not saltwater. This is simply something I am feeling on my skin. I hear the first mate yelling at me but I am not the first mate. His voice is simply something I can hear with my ears.

Sight. Sound. Taste. Touch. Smell. These are the five senses. I would argue that our mind is another sense organ. Our mind's job is to take the input coming into the brain and create thoughts from it. Our mind creates thoughts so that we can understand what is happening around us. However, we treat our mind differently than the other senses. I know I am not the guitar that I see. I know that I am not the guitar that I hear. When I make a mistake playing the guitar, however, my mind creates the thought, "You are awful at guitar," and I believe that I am this thought. Without even questioning it, I believe that I should give up on guitar just because that's the information my mind created.

I do think it's time for a shift. My mind creates thoughts so that life makes sense. I am not my thoughts. I do not have to believe the thoughts that my mind creates.

"I should go to the pantry and eat all of the chocolate chips."

That's just a thought. I am not obligated to do that. (Though I might choose to.)

"Why did you make that mistake? You are so stupid."

This is just a thought. I do not have to believe it.

As it turns out, 20-year-old Danielle was an awesome sailor. You should be so lucky to have her at the helm during 15 foot seas. She did not know that she had a choice about her thoughts. She was walking on the unconsciously easy path in the forest of her mind.

No more, I say! From this day forth, we shall be aware of our thoughts as just thoughts. We shall not become our thoughts.

We shall choose the path through the forest that is the most beneficial for us, even if it is more challenging.

For now, let's focus on simply being aware of our thoughts. In future chapters, we will revisit this topic and delve a bit deeper.

~~LIFE LESSON #3: I must eat chocolate.~~
Well.....true but not quite what I was aiming for.
LIFE LESSON #3: You are not your thoughts.

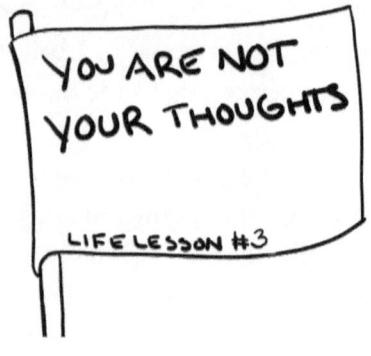

Chapter Summary

- Our brains are composed of special cells called neurons. There are 80-100 billion neurons in a human brain.
- Neurons can connect to each other to create specific pathways. Each unique pathway creates a different thought or action.
- The thoughts that we have most often become strong pathways in our brains. These thoughts will start playing in the backgrounds of our minds automatically.
- We are capable of changing our thoughts but it can feel uncomfortable and challenging.
- Our mind is another sense organ, similar to our eyes, ears, and nose. Our mind creates thoughts to help us make sense of our environments.
- You are not your thoughts. When your mind creates a thought, you get to choose whether to act on or believe that thought.

To Do List

- Can you think of any thoughts that you have often, maybe in the background of your life? Make a list of these thoughts. Which ones do you want to keep? Are there any that you would like to get rid of?
- As you go through your day, try to be more aware of your thoughts. Can you catch any of them passing quickly through the background? Are you able to pause and notice a thought instead of automatically reacting to it?
- Choose 1:
  - Draw an illustration of a forest with several paths in it. Some paths can be large and wide while others are tiny and narrow. Label the paths with thoughts. Write thoughts

you currently have on the large paths. Write thoughts you want to start cultivating on the narrow paths.

- Make a chart with two columns. In the first column, list negative thoughts that you would like to change. In the second column, rewrite those thoughts in a more positive way. (For example, instead of "You are horrible at steering the ship", I could change this to "You are so brave to not give up on a difficult task.")

4

Your Brakes Are Broken

I Have a Favorite Student

Noooo, I don't. Teachers aren't allowed to have a favorite student. That wouldn't be fair or something like that.

I do have a Top 5.

Let me tell you about a solid member of my Top 5 List. Her name is Bree. Well, no, her name is not Bree but I'm going to call her Bree because it is Irish for "fierce power" and that's a pretty good description of her. Also, I'm hoping she doesn't read this book because if she doesn't like what I am about to write, she will totally hunt me down. No person in their right mind would NOT be at least a little scared of Bree.

Let me tell you about Bree. At least the version of her that I taught in 7th and 8th grade, many years ago. Picture this:

Bree's natural facial expression is one of angry disgust. When you look at her, you automatically think one of the following things:

- Do I have toilet paper trailing off my shoe?
- Is she mad at me?
- Is she about to attack someone?
- How quickly can I slip into the classroom to hide?

Bree is opinionated. She will tell you exactly what she is thinking the moment she is thinking it. She does not use a lot of adjectives. Instead, she uses short, clear, concise language that cuts straight to the point.

I hate this.

This assignment is ridiculous.

Your face is stupid.

I think you get the point. Anyway, I'm not saying Bree is bad. No no no. Have we learned nothing? There is no such thing as good or bad. Bree is just Bree. She has these characteristics. As her teacher, I watched these characteristics play out in a few different scenarios, some that increased the happiness of those around her and some that did, let's say, quite the opposite.

Bree Example #1: We were having a "fresh air break" between classes. Several of the boys in the class were tossing a football back and forth. Another group, including Bree, were lounging on the picnic tables talking about Why Don't We (boy band) and fighting over who was the cutest.

One of the boys tossed the football and it flew off course towards the picnic table. It hits Bree on the leg.

The moment it happens, the world stops spinning and everyone turns to see what will happen next.

I don't think she actually growled but that is how my imagination plays the scene back to me. The boy who threw it jogged over and apologized to Bree. Bree picks up the football and, at point blank range, wound up with all her fierce might and threw the football at his face.

Yikes.

Bree Example #2: For this flashback, we find ourselves at lunch break. Several students are sitting at a table. The conversation flows in a very adolescent-y way, that is to say, incredibly randomly. At some point, the topic floats to something inappropriate. One student chooses to make fun of a particular group in society. He does unflattering impressions and uses hurtful language.

This time, no one sees it coming but nothing can hold back the righteous anger of Bree. Bree rises up, as if expanding in size, and lets this boy and the group have it. When the boy tries to talk back, Bree cuts him off and puts him in his place.

When Bree feels she is finished, she stalks over to me, gives me the quick summary, tells me that she knows she was rude but that she doesn't care if she gets in trouble because she couldn't stand there and let them talk like that.

I could have walked over and addressed the situation but I did not have to. Bree had completely taken care of it.

Superhero or Supervillain?

Do you see why I love Bree? She has the fiery power to change the world around her. She cares intensely about justice and treating others fairly. She is confident and loud about speaking up for what is right in this world. When Bree runs for President, I will be the first to vote for her.

Although, on the other hand, she gets mad really quickly. She doesn't think twice about hitting or kicking someone if she thinks they deserve it. She can be rude and hurt people's feelings when she talks without thinking.

Bree is, in summary, either a glorious superhero or a dastardly supervillain. At any moment throughout the day, she has the power to save the world or to destroy it.

Isn't that interesting.

The truth is that the same is true of all of us. I have both a superhero and a supervillain just waiting to rise up inside of me. Depending on my day and on my mood, either could surface. Fortunately or unfortunately, this never ending battle between good and evil is much more drastic in adolescents. Events will trigger you into superhero action much faster than they will in me, a boring adult. Similarly, you will spiral into a supervillain mode at the slightest offense whereas I can withstand that temptation much longer.

There is a reason for this. A very good reason. A scientifically proven and excellent reason. Allow me to enlighten you. <insert evil laugh here>

Brains Are Cool

Do you have any idea how magnificent the human brain is? It's wild. Your brain has a texture of firm jelly, which is an awesomely gross fact. It weighs, on average, about 3 pounds. (The same amount as my optimal daily chocolate intake.) Information can speed through your brain at up to 250 miles per hour. There are about 100,000 miles of blood vessels in and throughout the brain. Shall I go on or are you impressed yet?

There is so much information about the brain that I could write a book (or two or three) just on that topic. For right now, we are just going to dip our toes into the topic of cool brain stuff. The brain has different areas that specialize in a variety of tasks. Let me tell you in general about two areas and then I'll explain why your brain is currently wackadoodle.

There are two parts of the brain that work together to help us to process and to react to life events. The amygdala is the part of the brain that is responsible for generating emotions in response to situations. A football hits Bree in the leg. Bree's amygdala processes this information and tells Bree to become the Incredible Hulk in response.

Luckily, we have the prefrontal cortex to balance out the amygdala. The prefrontal cortex (PFC) is the very calm and reasonable alter ego to the Incredible Hulk. The PFC is, in fact, like Bruce Banner. It is the area of the brain that allows you to plan, organize information, and make decisions based on current information. Very practical. When my friend yells at me and I feel that wave of anger wash over me, the PFC is what tells me that she actually had a really bad day at work, so I should be compassionate and show kindness instead.

The amygdala reacts to events but the PFC moderates those reactions and helps us to change those reactions before we regret them. That is how it works in adults (most of them, anyway).

You are not an adult. You are an adolescent. Your brain does not work this way.

AMYGDALA | PRE-FRONTAL CORTEX

The amygdala is responsible for all the emotional ups and down you feel (Incredible Hulk) while the pre-frontal cortex is the very calm and reasonable alter ego (Bruce Banner).

Your Brain Is Weird

First, let's address pruning and I'm not talking about your fingers in the pool in the summer. After you are born, your brain starts to accumulate information quickly. You are learning more about your environment, learning language, learning how to move. It's very exciting. Your brain grows and the neural connections in your brain expand.

This continues to happen, more or less, until you hit adolescence, between the ages of 12-14. At this point, your brain is no longer interested in accumulating more and more information. Your brain wants to become efficient. Having a ton of information is pretty cool but that means it takes longer for information to travel through the brain. At this point, your brain decides that it will get rid of information that is not being used. That way, only the super important information is left and it can become faster and more efficient at using this information.

This process is called pruning. Just like a gardener will remove branches that are not useful or are in the way, your brain removes neurons that are not being used. They're unused, therefore they are not needed, therefore they are bogging us down, therefore they must go!

While you spent the first part of your life accumulating more and more knowledge, you are now doing the opposite. You are losing knowledge. Do you ever feel forgetful? Like you can't remember something that you really think you know? Ya, that's pruning. I once saw my adolescent daughter standing at the kitchen sink holding her empty bowl of cereal. I had asked her to wash her bowl. She literally could not remember how to do that. Pruning.

During adolescence, pruning is happening in your prefrontal cortex. You know, the part that helps you to organize, plan, and make practical decisions. The next time your parents com-

During pruning, neurons for skills that you no longer use are removed (tossed into the garbage). Neurons for skills that you use often are strengthened and preserved.

plain about your lack of organization or the fact that you just did NOT think things through well, you can blame it on pruning. (But don't tell them I told you to say that.)

While your PFC is under construction and not fully accessible, your amygdala is totally mature. You are able to feel ALL the emotions and you feel them strongly. Herein lies the problem: You have intensely strong emotions but you do not have the ability to think about them, process them, or make wise decisions about them.

Think of it this way:

Pretend you are riding your bike downhill. Since you are riding downhill, you will naturally speed up and start to go faster and faster. Luckily, your bike has brakes. If you start to gather too much speed, you can squeeze the brakes and slow down to a more comfortable level.

Make sense?

Good - let's apply it to your brain.

In this scenario, the downhill speed is like your amygdala and the brakes are like your PFC. As life events happen and you head downhill, your bike picks up speed and you experience large, and sometimes wild, emotions. At this point, an adult would pump the brakes and slow the bike down. They would use their PFC to process the emotion, put it into perspective, and decide on an appropriate response. But you're not an adult. Your PFC is under construction, which is to say that your brakes are broken. You are careening downhill, feeling every single emotion, but you have no brakes to slow things down. The emotions are out of control and your PFC is not able to help you to sort through things. You react to life based on the strength of your emotions, because you have no brakes to slow things down for you.

Case in point: The football hits Bree in the leg. In an adult, they might feel an initial wave of anger but then they would see the boy running towards them apologizing for what happened. The adult's PFC would organize the information and provide the rationale behind what happened. "Oh - he didn't mean to hit me. It was an accident and he is sorry that it happened." Instead of throwing the football directly into his face, the adult might smile and toss the football back to him. As for Bree? She doesn't have a working PFC so all she felt was an intense wave of anger. Her brain was not able to make sense of it for her, so she simply reacted to the anger without thinking about what that might mean. Supervillain.

This process happening in your brain starts around the ages 12-14 and, I hate to be the one to inform you, lasts until you are 25 or so. Remember 20-year-old Danielle who was steering the ship through crazy weather? Yup, an adolescent.

Take a moment to check in with yourself. Have you ever felt an incredibly intense emotion and you reacted without thinking? Perhaps you yelled ridiculously at someone or even physically reacted to them?

This does not have to be all negative. Let's switch the reaction. Have you ever had something good happen and you were so weirdly and incredibly happy for a little while? Have you ever found something so silly that you laughed and laughed and laughed about it while your parents stood and stared at you as if you were an alien?

Have you ever heard your parents or other adults whisper about how dramatic those teens are being right now <eye roll>?

Yaaaaa...it's true. Welcome to adolescence.

Why You Should Read This Book

Finally, at the end of Chapter 4, I am ready to tell you why you should read this book. It all comes down to your weird, under construction brain.

According to Life Lesson #1, sometimes life sucks. Truly, my friend. Guess what? Because of your low functioning PFC, you feel all of the suckiness without having a reliable way to process all of it. When you experience a Pink Panty Incident, you are likely to respond in a supervillain sort of way. At the very least, you will react un-optimally and create more unhappiness for yourself.

Because you don't have the ability to really slow down and think things through, you grasp happy things with a grip that feels impossible to loosen. You avoid unhappy things as if your life depended on it. Well, isn't that interesting. Yes, that's right, Life Lesson #2 comes into play. It really is interesting but only if you are able to slow down long enough to have that perspective. When you are riding your bike downhill on a dirt path through the mountainous desert, you don't have enough time to even think about the idea of something being interesting. Your eyes are wide as you see the HUGE spines on the cacti lining the dirt path and wondering how you are going to make that turn up ahead without any brakes. There are many words flying through your brain, but interesting is not one of them.

It only takes one time being thrown from your bike into a cactus plant for you to assume that every single time you are riding downhill, you will probably get attacked by cacti. You probably start to think that you are a terrible cyclist. Truly, the worse. It's all your fault. Mmm-hmm. Life Lesson #3. Our minds create thoughts and, unfortunately, we tend to believe these thoughts.

With a brain that is determined to hold onto these types of dramatically negative thoughts, how can you ever actually be happy?

Aha! Welcome to my book.

This book, essentially, is about understanding the constructs of life and how to become more aware of your reactions to life so that you can reach the Dalai Lama's preferred state of happiness.

By the time you are 25 or so, your PFC will have matured and you will be able to process information and make rational decisions. Kind of. Well, a majority of the time. Maybe.

There is a shortcut though.

There are two ways to slow down whilst careening downhill on a bicycle. You can pump the brakes. That's one method. You could also turn off the downhill path and ride a path that is more even, thereby slowing down naturally and without the use of brakes.

This book is about how to find that shortcut.

That shortcut is called mindfulness.

LIFE LESSON #4: Buy a new bike.

Give me a minute. I'll get it.

LIFE LESSON #4: Mindfulness is the answer.

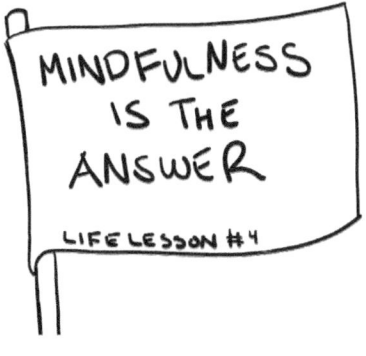

Chapter Summary

- I don't have a favorite student (supposedly) but I do have a Top 5 List. (This is just useful information for any of my students out there reading this. I accept bribes of dark chocolate.)
- The amygdala is the part of the brain that is responsible for the intense emotions that you feel.
- The prefrontal cortex (PFC) is the part of the brain that helps you to organize information, process events, and make rational decisions.
- Adolescence is a period of time starting around the age of 12-14 and lasting until about 25.
- During adolescence, the PFC is under construction and not functioning optimally although the amygdala is fully mature.
- As a result of this, you have intensely strong emotions but you do not have the ability to think about them, process them, or make wise decisions about them.
- You should read this book because it will solve all of your problems.

To Do List

- Can you think of a time when you were a Superhero? How about a Supervillain? Make a list of 3 situations for each category.
- I came up with the metaphor of the adolescent brain being similar to riding a bike downhill with broken brakes. Come up with your own metaphor for the way the amygdala and the PFC function during adolescence. Share your metaphor as either an illustration or in a written format.
- Create a short video in the format of a nature documentary. Instead of narrating a study of the red panda or the blue-footed booby, pretend that you are studying the fascinating or-

ganism called the Adolescent. What would you need the viewers at home to understand about this species?

Part II

In which I get to the point already.

5

The Genie Will Destroy You

Let's revisit the true self. Hiding in the cave behind your heart. Because you covered it up over the years, not wanting anyone else to see it.

Revisit the example: I go surfing. I inexplicably catch a wave. I feel supreme awesomeness for 5 seconds. Ah, my true self. Free of doubt, worry, or limitations. Just calmly happy.

The thing is, I no longer live at the beach anymore. In fact, I live landlocked, not an ocean in sight. Not even a lake. Alas, I cannot go surfing anymore. Now what am I going to do to find that feeling?

Well, let's break it down. What is actually happening when I go surfing and find my true self? In those precious moments, I am not thinking. I am not questioning how to catch a wave. I am not worried about wiping out or about the possible sharks waiting for me beneath the surface. I am not overthinking how to paddle correctly. I'm not even doubting my ability to actually do that.

Ohhh....now I see. When I feel like my true self, I am not caught up in my thoughts. I am not stuck in any negative thought paths in my neural forest. I am not grasping towards catching the wave and I am not trying to avoid wiping out. In those moments, nothing is labeled as "good" or "bad". I'm just alive. In that specific moment. No more, no less.

And that, right there, solves the world's problems. Yes, I would be grateful and humbled to accept the Nobel Prize for Awesomeness. It was a long journey to get here and I have several acknowledgements. First of all, chocolate. Secondly, my new pair of boots.

What's that?

You have no idea what I'm talking about?

I'm getting ahead of myself?

I don't need a new pair of boots?

Well that's a lot to throw at a person all at one time.

Fine. Let's backtrack. But know this and know it well: I'm keeping the boots.

The key to reconnecting with our true self lies in our thoughts. For most of us, we spend our days completely caught up in our thoughts. Even though our mind creates thoughts based on input from the other senses, we tend to go right along with them. We react to our thoughts with emotions, which then create more thoughts, which we then react to with more emotions. And that's all before breakfast.

We grasp and avoid things, trying so hard to be happy. But these actions simply create more thoughts to which we grasp harder or avoid more intensely. More thoughts and emotions follow. Now we're up to lunch.

We allow the same negative thoughts to travel unconsciously through our minds all day long. You're not good enough. Look at what you've done now. Or, I'm the best in this room, how dare they question me. We have traveled these neural pathways so often that we don't even recognize we are having these thoughts. They shape how we view the world. They lead to more thoughts and emotions. We made it to dinnertime.

As you can see, over the course of a normal day, my true self has not been in control at all. My true self has not made a single appearance or a single decision. I have spent my time wrapped up in the thoughts that my mind has created as I try ever so hard to find that elusive happiness.

The only time that I can remember who I truly am is when my thoughts are not controlling me.

The pathway to this goal is so simple. It lies in plain sight and yet it is dastardly challenging. The only way to not be caught up in thoughts is to be in the present moment.

Try it. In this specific moment, what do you smell? Look up. What do you immediately see? What colors? Be specific. What sounds do you hear? Where are they coming from? What can you feel?

Did you notice it? When you quickly focused on the specific senses and what they were immediately aware of, you were not creating thoughts. You were not grasping or avoiding, you were simply noticing. Perhaps it only lasted a few moments. Perhaps you noticed everything ("I smell salmon") and then found yourself immediately shifting into thoughts ("Ew, I hate seafood"). That's ok. What's important is that you had even the briefest moment of not being caught in thoughts.

It is in this state that the thoughts no longer control us. When the thoughts no longer control us, the true self emerges.

And we live happily ever after.

The End.

Not The End

Just kidding. If it were that easy, I wouldn't get to write a book about it. (Or accept a Nobel Prize in Awesomeness. Or meet Oprah because she loves my book. Or buy new boots to meet Oprah because she loves my book.)

This practice of bringing ourselves to the present moment, in an effort to remove ourselves from the control of our thoughts, is called mindfulness.

Grab a scrap of paper and a pencil.

Now, quickly, without thinking or overthinking, what images or words come to mind when you see/hear the word mindfulness? Write them down.

It is quite interesting the thoughts we have about mindfulness. Some of them are determined by what we have overheard others say. Many are determined by social media and advertising.

Here are some examples of what people have told me they think of when they think mindfulness:

- Zero thoughts
- Sitting still
- Eyes closed
- Feeling peaceful
- Nothing bothers you
- Cross-legged
- Empty mind

The media, images in magazines, and social media would have us believe that these are the words that describe mindfulness. Thou shalt sit in a cross-legged position with a peaceful expression on your face whilst thou empties the mind completely of any thoughts. Only then will thou feel calm and never suffer again. Also, it would help if thou wore really trendy leggings or a white tunic. Incense burning in the background is a must.

For the record, I love burning incense. Also, I own more leggings than cool boots. (Seems like a mistake.) I am not judging any of the above statements. What I am saying is that the image described above portrays only one pathway to mindfulness. This is the inaccuracy. There are, in fact, as many ways to practice mindfulness as there are leggings in my closet.

Don't Take the Genie

What is the path? How do we find our way to mindfulness?

First, a story. This is an old Indian story that has been told in many different ways. Here is my version.

Once upon a time, a man was walking down a road when he was passed by another man who was holding a genie. Intrigued, the man asked about the genie.

"Will he really do anything you want?" the man asked.

The other man looked at him wearily.

"Oh yes," he replied.

The first man could not determine why he did not seem happier about this.

"Can I have the genie?" he asked on a whim.

The second man agreed. As he passed over the genie, he warned the man.

"He will do anything you want but when you run out of things for the genie to do, he will destroy you."

With that ominous message, the second man went on his way.

The man, now with a genie, was very excited! He had so many different things for the genie to do. True to his word, the genie did all of them. The man would write list after list of chores, and the genie attended to all of them.

Over time, the man's lists grew shorter and shorter. He was running out of tasks for the genie to do. As this happened, the man remembered the warning and suddenly became scared. Would the genie destroy him if he ran out of tasks?

Out of fear, the man searched for a great teacher who might guide him in his treacherous situation. He told the teacher his plight and asked for advice.

"Build a pole in your yard and tell the genie to run up and down it."

The man hurriedly did so. To this day, the genie is running up and down the pole and the man is happily living his life.

This story perfectly describes the goal of mindfulness. In this story, the genie represents our mind. We can give our mind different jobs to do. Unload the dishwasher. Solve the algebra system of equations. Read Danielle's awesome book. While the mind is engaged in a task, it is focused and we are very happy. The moment we run out of tasks for the mind to do, however, it starts to create thoughts. It urges us to grasp and to avoid. It pelts us with unhelpful thoughts. It tells us stories that we automatically believe. To be very dramatic, it tries to destroy us (our true selves), just like the genie.

So, just like with the genie, we know what we have to do. Give the genie a job to do. In our case, give the mind a job to do. The beautifully meditating people wearing leggings and burning incense on social media are doing just that. They are telling the mind, "Focus on the breath." Then, the mind will focus on the breath and, since it is doing that, it will not create thoughts in which we can get caught.

For many years, mindfulness was taught just like how we see on social media. Sit cross-legged. Close the eyes. Just breathe. Because of this, most people now think that this is the only way to practice mindfulness.

Uh, hello, so not true.

For some people, when they sit still and focus on the breath, their minds go haywire and create even more thoughts.

"Can I remember how to breathe? Am I breathing right? OMG, what if I accidentally stop breathing?"

For these people, focusing on the breath is not optimal. It does not succeed at what we are trying to do. Remember, the goal of mindfulness is to stop being controlled by the mind and its thoughts. There are so many different ways that this can happen. Just a few examples: gardening, surfing, playing an instrument, and coloring.

Why Aren't the Thoughts Going Away?

Remember Bree? A member of my Top 5 Student List? One day, after practicing mindfulness in class, she threw a book across the room and yelled loudly at no one and everyone, "It's not helping! There are too many thoughts!"

I'll be honest. Bree has a point.

Too. Many. Thoughts.

This is the number one reason why people quit mindfulness. They see the social media posts; they buy leggings and incense; they sit down and meditate. A week later, they wave the white flag and tell their friends that mindfulness just wasn't for them. When I have talked to these people and inquired about why they did not like mindfulness, the answer is along the lines of:

"I thought mindfulness was going to make me super calm. I thought it would take away all of the crazy thoughts. It did the opposite. I feel like I'm having more thoughts than when I started."

Ah, my inner Yoda says in response, you must unlearn what you have learned.

The point of mindfulness is to stop being controlled by our thoughts. The point is not to get rid of the thoughts. Remember that the mind's job is to create thoughts. It will always do this. What we want to do is to stop believing everything the mind tells us. We want to see the thought, acknowledge it, and then make a decision about it.

Do you like movies? I love going to the movie theater. Comedies? Yes. Adventures? Always. Horror? No. No horror movies, you've gone too far. Think of the thoughts as if you are sitting in a movie theater. The movie is playing and you are enjoying the show. You are not a character in the movie. You know this. You can watch the events without getting tricked into thinking you are the one experiencing the events.

We want to view our thoughts the same way. When we are caught in our thoughts, we believe everything they tell us. We feel the emotions intensely as if they are 100% the absolute truth. We are on the emotional roller coaster. What if, instead of this, we could view our thoughts as if we are watching them appear on a screen at the movie theater? We see the thoughts but there is some space. We are not the thoughts. We are just watching them. Like an interesting movie.

This is what happens during mindfulness. The thoughts do not disappear but we are choosing not to engage with them. They are just floating around on the movie screen. Just as one scene in a movie ends and another begins, one thought will end and make way for another.

When people first start practicing mindfulness, they are often surprised at just how many thoughts they are having! They never realized before because in the past they were so caught up in their thoughts. When beginners think they are failing because they are having "more" thoughts, what is happening is that they are simply becoming aware of their thoughts for the first time.

Isn't that interesting?

Yes, my friend, it is very interesting.

Every time you sit down (or stand up, or twirl in a circle) to practice mindfulness, think to yourself, "I wonder what type of movie will show up in my thoughts today." Then let those thoughts play out in the movie theater in your head.

As long as you realize that you are not trying to get rid of your thoughts, you'll be much better able to work with them.

As we move through the next chapters of the book, we will uncover different methods of achieving mindfulness. Like a pair of boots, my advice is to try them on and see if they fit. You will discover the methods that work well for you (olive green clog boots) as well as the ones that, well, do not (stilettos - ow).

LIFE LESSON #5: The genie will destroy you.
Hehe. Maybe. But let's try different phrasing.
LIFE LESSON #5: The present moment is where it's at.

And a bonus life lesson:
LIFE LESSON #6: Horror movies are too scary.
True statement.
LIFE LESSON #6: Don't resist. Coexist. (with your thoughts, that is)

Chapter Summary

- Remember: the purpose of life is to remember who we really are.
- When we get caught in the thoughts, we start grasping, avoiding, and labeling. All of these activities cover up the true self.
- One day, I will buy new boots before meeting Oprah.
- We can remove ourselves from being captured by the thoughts by shifting our attention to the present moment. We do this by focusing on exactly what is happening around us at this specific moment.
- The practice of mindfulness involves giving the mind a job to do. When the mind is focused on something, such as breathing, it is not creating thoughts in which we get caught.
- There are many ways to practice mindfulness. Any activity in which your mind is focused on one task and you are not caught up in the thoughts is mindfulness.
- Our mind creates thoughts. It will always do this.
- The purpose of mindfulness is not to get rid of the thoughts. The purpose of mindfulness is to not get caught in the thoughts.

To Do List

- Bell of Mindfulness. Set several alarms on your phone (with calming alarm sounds) to go off several times a day. You can also download apps to do this same thing. Every time the alarm sounds, practice coming to the present moment. Move yourself out of your thoughts and focus on what your senses are telling you. (Do this at school. Your teachers will love it.)
- There are two main, very big lessons from this chapter. Lessons to NEVER forget. For the rest of your life. Big deal. 1) Coming to the present moment can get you out of your

thoughts. 2) You are not trying to eliminate your thoughts. You are trying to coexist with them. Use these rules and choose one option:

- Create a pamphlet about the dangers of "mindlessness". Be dramatic. Embellish. Be ridiculous. And then give the solutions to the problem (the two rules).
- Write a script for a movie trailer about mindfulness. Write it in one of these genres: romance movie, comedy, or tragedy. Include the two rules. Then, film the trailer!
- Draw a comic strip of Captain Mindfulness versus The Ghastly Genie. Who will overcome? Probably the one who remembers the two rules.

6

Prepare to Be Boggled

I'm Having Issues

I am in a state of overwhelm. There are too many things for me to tell you. I literally do not know where to start. Maybe I'll just sit here and pretend I'm writing a book. If I tap my fingers lightly on the keys of the laptop, it will even sound like I am doing work. Literally, no one will ever know. Maybe we don't need an entire book on mindfulness. Maybe five chapters is enough. You have enough info to get you through life, right? Will a publisher even print half of a book? What if I tell them it's the whole book? They probably don't read ALL of the stuff they're sent right? I could get away with it. Seems easier than figuring out how to write this chapter.

<Empty stare.>

<Forlorn glance into the blankness of my future.>

<Slowly dissolves into a puddle of indecision on the ground.>

Several chocolate bars hours later...

I've decided I should really just explain myself.

This chapter is about science. And mindfulness. This chapter is about the science of mindfulness. OMG, you have no idea. Science is my first love. When I'm in the realm of science, everything makes sense. As for mindfulness? Mindfulness is my true

true love. Mindfulness saved me and changed the direction of my life. It allows me to be calm enough, sane enough, and happy enough to enjoy my first love, science.

In this chapter, I will be combining science and mindfulness. My two huge loves are coming together in a fusion of staggering proportions and I don't even know if I can contain myself.

I just realized.

I will also be talking about adolescents. My absolute favorite people on earth, perhaps even the galaxy (PERHAPS even the universe). I will be talking about adolescent brain science and why mindfulness is super fantastically incredibly important for this age group.

Science + mindfulness + adolescents

I can't even.

I need to take a lap. It's just too much.

One pair of boots day later...

I'm ready.

Prepare yourself for an astounding amalgamation of quintessential guidance towards the sublime boggling of your mind.

The Spy of the Body

Let's think about your school classroom. In every classroom, there is one person who takes charge of most things. Plans the lessons. Watches you as you work (creepy). Reacts to situations that happen. Operates silently in the background, doing things that you aren't even aware of.

The teacher. I'm talking about the teacher.

She/he/they are like the boss. The Captain of the Millennium Falcon (ask your parents). Both T'Challa and Shuri of Wakanda (throw some Okoye in there too). Albus Percival Wulfric Brian Dumbledore of Hogwarts (get the man a lemon drop).

My point is that your teacher is crazy busy, always juggling ten tasks at one time. Your teacher does things that you are aware of but she/he/they are also managing about ten times ten tasks that you will never even know about. Things that make the classroom run smoothly but that are not obvious.

You know what, we all need to pause. Go write an email to your teacher right now and say thank you.

I'll wait.

Did you write it in complete sentences? You know your teachers get righteously annoyed when you don't. Go rewrite.

Ok, let's continue.

Your teacher and your classroom are very similar to the nervous system, which is the exciting science thing that will lead into mindfulness and eventually link up with adolescents. <Chills>

The nervous system is a component of the body that is often referred to as the control center. It sends signals throughout the body and controls movements, thoughts, and bodily actions. Breathing, talking, the beating of your heart, responding to danger, playing piano, reading, trying on new boots, kicking classmates who hit you with a football. All of these are controlled by the nervous system.

You'll notice that, in that list above, some of those activities are voluntary, as in you choose to do them: talking, playing piano, kicking classmates. Other activities happen involuntarily, as in you don't have to think about it for them to happen: breathing, the beating of your heart, trying on new boots (I swear it just happens). These form two different parts of the nervous system. The somatic nervous system controls conscious actions, those things that you actively choose to do. The autonomic nervous system controls the unconscious actions, like the contraction of your intestines to move food along your digestive tract. (So happy I don't have to think about that all day.)

It's this super secret autonomic nervous system that we will focus on. The autonomic system is totally the spy of the body. Keeping tabs on all the unconscious activities. Slipping by unnoticed. Always watching and reporting back to the brain with intel from the body. It's a total Elf on the Shelf meets Jason Bourne situation.

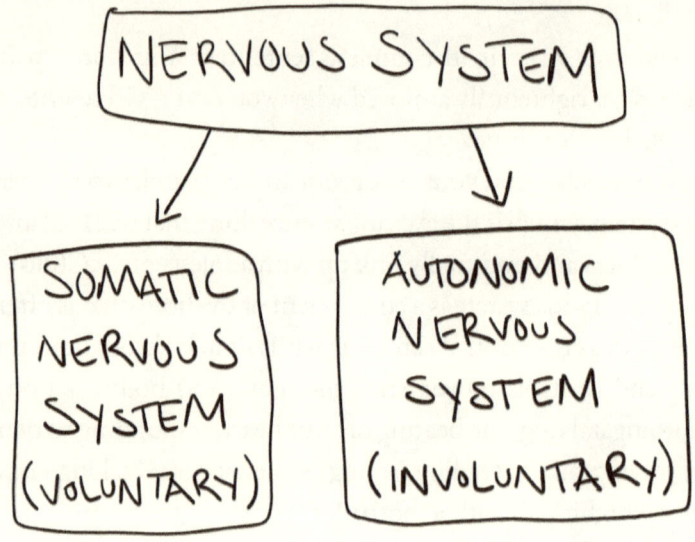

The Double Agent

If the autonomous nervous system is a spy, then it is a double agent. There are two parts of the autonomous system: the sympathetic nervous system (SNS) and the parasympathetic nervous system (PNS).

The sympathetic nervous system is the part of the nervous system that is very kind and is a great listener. No, just kidding. That's the gallbladder. Being serious, the SNS is called the Fight or Flight system. It takes control of bodily functions that will help you react in a dangerous situation. This is when Jason

Bourne realizes he is being chased so he drives down a flight of stairs to escape.

As a good spy, at the first sign of danger, the SNS prepares you for what's coming. Your heart rate speeds up, blood pressure increases, pupils dilate, and you start sweating. Are you excited or anxious? Could be both. Either way, you are now ready to either fight the enemy or take flight (run away) from the enemy. This reaction will happen under any perceived threat, whether that threat requires actual fighting/running or not. For example, you will react like this in a physical fight, but you will also react like this when you walk into math class without your homework and the teacher calls on you to answer the first question.

Stress = Sympathetic Nervous System

After every high intensity spy job, all good spies have to disappear for a while. You know, go off the grid. Take a break and relax in a lavish hut in a tropical location. Perhaps a little sunbathing. Sailing. Maybe some snorkeling or even parasailing. Yeah, this is the life. Totally relaxing and forgetting about all those stressful times.

This is the parasympathetic nervous system (PNS). The PNS is also called the Rest & Digest system. Your heart rate slows down, blood pressure lowers, digestion increases, and you feel an overall sense of calm. Think of parasympathetic as parasailing. Just gliding through the air behind a boat. Enjoying beautiful scenery. Not a care in the world.

Every little thing's going to be alright = Parasympathetic Nervous System

Only one system can be "in charge" at one time. If one system is activated, the other is running in the background. Check in right now. Which system do you think is in control? Do you feel stressed or a little anxious? That means the SNS is prevalent.

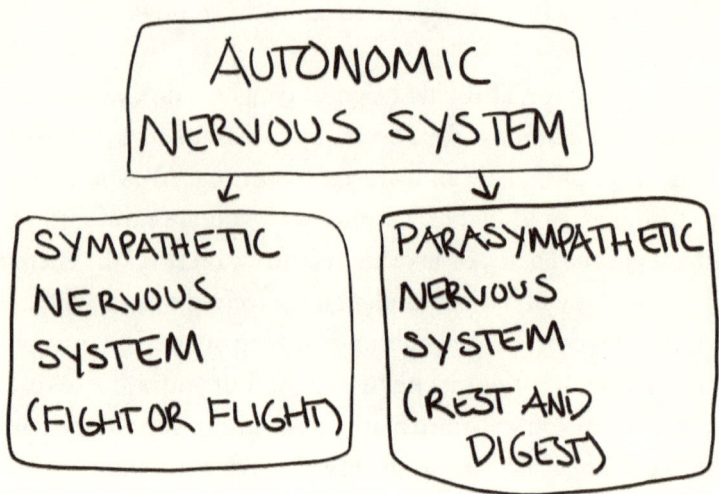

Do you feel totally relaxed and calm? That means the PNS has taken over.

Let's take it one step further. Think about your typical day. If you were to guess, what % of time do you spend with the SNS in control (stressed) and what % of the time do you spend with the PNS in control (relaxed)? What do you think those percentages are for your parents? How about for a stockbroker on Wall Street? A soccer fanatic who is watching their favorite team compete in the World Cup? Your teacher who is simultaneously teaching, taking attendance, managing behavior, keeping everyone in a good mood, and doing all of that in grandiose style? (Go thank your teacher again. For real.)

Research has found that a majority of people spend most of their time with an activated SNS system. In other words, their bodies are prepared to fight or flight all day long. Not fun! Not only does being in this state feel edgy and stressful, it also negatively impacts our physical health.

What do you think is the optimal combination of SNS and PNS? Is it a 50/50 situation? What if we got rid of the SNS all together? Do we really need it? I mean, all it does is make me feel anxious.

Turns out that, even though SNS activation can feel uncomfortable, we can't just get rid of it. The SNS is what gives us motivation and energy to do daily activities. If we removed it, we would sit on the couch, feel relaxed, but not accomplish anything at all. The optimal combo is:

Mainly PNS activation so that we feel comfortable and peaceful.

Mild SNS activation to give us a sense of enthusiasm and energy to do our daily activities.

Occasionally SNS spikes so that we can deal with demanding or dangerous situations.

Let's Go Parasailing

I feel exhilarated after talking about that science. I'm guessing you feel the same. How could you not?? I'm about to take it to the next level by bringing in the topic of mindfulness. Take a breath and prepare yourself.

Mindfulness is that state of mind where we are not traveling the crazy train of our thoughts, we are here in the present moment, and we feel (mostly) calm. We are very aware of everything around us.

In those times when we are on the crazy train, we are grasping and avoiding.

"I NEED NEW BOOTS. MUST ACQUIRE NEW BOOTS RIGHT NOW!"

Or...

"I CAN'T GO BACK TO THE DENTIST. THEY ARE GOING TO POKE MY GUMS WITH SCARY INSTRUMENTS. MUST AVOID THE DENTIST!"

Both of these situations, grasping and avoiding, activate the SNS. It is stressful to want something so badly or to avoid something intensely. You are fighting for something or you are running away from something. No thank you.

Pulling out of this state of mind can happen by reading and practicing philosophical ideas and thoughts about life (Part I of this book, for example). The last Life Lesson in Part I gives us another way that we can shift. This lesson indicates that mindfulness is the answer. And so it is. As it turns out, the practice of mindfulness naturally activates your PNS.

At this point, there have been several research studies that support the idea of mindfulness. People who have a mindfulness practice have experienced not only feelings of calm and peace but they have also experienced several positive health outcomes: lower blood pressure, lower anxiety, lower depression, improved concentration and focus. And that's just a partial list!

By practicing mindfulness, we are allowing our bodies to find that optimal nervous system activation: mostly PNS with a bit of SNS.

If you need me, I'll be parasailing over tropical waters...

But Wait - There's More

Hold on. I can't go parasailing yet. I need to fold in the last exciting aspect of this chapter.

Science + Mindfulness + Adolescents.

It's happpppppppening.

Why am I writing a book on mindfulness for adolescents? Not grown-ups. Not parents. Not teachers. You. Why do I care so much that you learn mindfulness practices?

The answer is threefold.

Firstfold Reason

Firstfoldly (most definitely a word), let's think back to Chapter 4 when we learned some adolescent brain science. Remember that you are careening downhill on a bicycle but you have no brakes. You have a fully functioning amygdala that feels every emotion. It reacts in a HUGE way to those emotions. Guess what system is involved in feeling really big emotions? Uh-huh, the good ol' SNS stressmaker.

Meanwhile, you do not have a mature prefrontal cortex that helps you to process those emotions. You simply feel overwhelmed by emotions and make decisions based on the feeling, instead of using reasoning as well.

It turns out that, during the adolescent years, the SNS in adolescents can be triggered by even small events. What might feel normal or slightly interesting to other age groups can feel like a massive event to an adolescent. You are more prone to stress right now than at any other age. Even the feeling of being super excited is a trigger for the SNS.

The practice of mindfulness naturally activates the PNS. When adolescents are in a state of relaxation, they can access their prefrontal cortex easier, they react slower to those large emotions, and the world starts to feel more manageable. Stress hormones decrease, anxiety/depression decrease, and they transform from the Incredible Hulk back into mild-mannered Bruce Banner.

Secondfold Reason

Secondfoldly (less sure that is a word), remember that the adolescent brain is undergoing the process of pruning. Neural pathways that are not being used will be removed so that the brain can be more efficient. Those tap dancing lessons you took when you were 7? Ya, you haven't tap danced since then, so those neurons are going away. Any neurons that are not used often will be removed while neurons that are being used will be strengthened. You do algebra every day? Don't worry - you can keep those critical thinking neurons.

This whole pruning thing has GIGANTIC implications for your life! The habits and patterns that you establish during adolescence (ages 12-25 ish) are the neurons that will become stronger. You are essentially setting yourself up for the rest of your life.

Case in point: boots. I told you in Chapter 2 that it was in my adolescent years that my grandparents started sending me money for my Christmas present. It was at this time that I became interested in boots and I would buy one pair of new boots every holiday with this money. This became a habit during adolescence. To this day, every holiday season, I get a craving for a new pair of boots.

You have a choice in these next years. You can set yourself up with some strong habits that will benefit you in the following decades of your life (like buying new boots). The opposite is true too. If you develop lots of unhealthy habits, these will tend to follow you in life as well. The choice is yours.

Now, you can totally change your habits. Don't panic. You won't ruin your life if you don't create every single positive habit that you need in your life during these important years. For example, my sister never created a habit of buying boots. Despite this, I know that if I counseled her during the upcoming holiday season, I would be able to help her change her ways. With enough hard work and dedication, she can change her boot neural pathways. The point is that adolescence is a powerful time inside your brain so you can harness the processes that are already happening and make them work in your favor. Your future self is begging you.

Not only does mindfulness calm and semi-control the angry Hulk inside of you, it is also creating positive neural pathways that will help you for the rest of your life!

Thirdfold Reason

Last but by no means least, we come to my thirdfold (definitely not a word) reason for you, an adolescent, to absolutely learn mindfulness. It has to do with that cave behind your heart. And your caveman ancestors.

Way back in the day, in the ultimate once upon a time, adolescence was the age at which individuals left the family group to set out on their own. Individuals who successfully did this were the ones who created their own families and reproduced to pass their genes (DNA) onto the next generation. Over the years, this desire to leave the family, explore the unknown, and create individual thoughts and opinions became part of human DNA.

To this day, adolescents crave time away from the family. They want to make their own decisions and be part of the world in very real and productive ways. As part of this, adolescents start having abstract thoughts about who they are and what their place is in this world. While young children are naturally in touch with their true selves, adolescents have a brain complex enough to think about the true self as they search for meaning in the world. Not only are they able to do this, but they really really want to. They are on a quest to discover their purpose and place in the world. (Translation: They are searching for the true self hiding in the cave behind the heart.)

The search for meaning is really a search for awareness. You have to be aware of what is happening around you in order to question it and assert yourself into life in a meaningful way. The search for awareness can only happen in the present moment where life is happening. Looking for the present moment, are you? The present moment is found in mindfulness.

Wrapping It Up Nicely For You

As an adolescent, you naturally start to think deep thoughts in order to determine your place in the world. Mindfulness practices enhance this by activating your PNS and by providing methods for you to be in the present moment. Simultaneously, you are creating a habit that will positively affect Future You.

Boom. Science, mindfulness, and adolescents.

You're welcome.

LIFE LESSON #7: Fourthfoldly, Danielle makes up a lot of words.

Seems true to me but that's more of a statement, not a lesson.

LIFE LESSON #7: Learn mindfulness NOW, adolescents.

Chapter Summary

- The nervous system controls movements, thoughts, and bodily functions. It is the control center of the body, much like your teacher is the control center of your classroom.
- The nervous system is broken into two parts: the somatic system and the autonomic system. The somatic system controls voluntary movements, which are things you choose to do, like throw a football or stuff a handful of M&Ms into your mouth. The autonomic system controls involuntary movements, which are things that happen without you thinking about them, like your heart beating or your stomach digesting M&Ms.
- The autonomic system is then divided into two parts: the sympathetic nervous system (SNS) and the parasympathetic nervous system (PNS).
- The SNS is the fight or flight system. It prepares you to survive dangerous or stressful situations, even if the situations are only dangerous in your mind.
- The PNS is the rest and digest system. It promotes relaxation and feelings of peace.
- The optimal combination of nervous system activation is mostly PNS activation to feel at ease, minimal SNS activation for enthusiasm and motivation, and occasional SNS spikes to help us survive stressful activities.
- Most people live predominantly in SNS activation. This is an agitated state that has many harmful emotional, mental, and physical health consequences.
- Mindfulness practices naturally activate the PNS. By practicing mindfulness, you increase your emotional, mental, and physical health.
- As an adolescent, mindfulness can help you to be more aware of your emotions. As a result, you will not react as intensely

to them. (You will spend more time as Bruce Banner and less time as the Incredible Hulk.)

- With pruning happening in the adolescent brain, this is an important time to set up lifestyle habits that you will want to strengthen and use the rest of your life. By learning mindfulness during this critical period, you are ensuring that you will carry this skill into your adult life.
- The adolescent stage (ages 12-25 ish) is marked by a need for the adolescent to learn new things, explore the world, and to start thinking about the meaning of life and their place in it. Mindfulness is an activity that enhances the process of finding purpose and meaning. It can help adolescents to rediscover their true selves hiding in the cave behind the heart.
- This science + mindfulness + adolescents chapter is the greatest thing Danielle has ever accomplished. She feels incredibly fulfilled now.

To Do List

- Sit down and think about your day. Your current day. This one right here. Has the SNS or PNS been more active today so far?
- Think about your favorite movie or book. Which characters are definitely stuck in SNS mode? Are there any characters who demonstrate PNS activation?
- Consider the process of pruning. Make a list of thoughts or habits that you would love to be pruned out of your neural network. What thoughts or habits would you like to take their place?
- Consider the SNS versus the PNS. Create memes showing how the SNS is like a supervillain for our well-being while the PNS is the superhero.
- Go thank your teacher for being a superhero.

- Create an infographic or poster showing how mindfulness can help with the following: PNS activation, the search for meaning, and the creation of positive habits.

7

Mindfulness Whilst Sitting

Don't Fall Asleep in Class

Let me tell you about my first exposure to mindfulness. We will have to rewind the clock to the year 1999 when I was a sophomore at Cornell University. You know how there are some classes you love in school and you wish everyone would just let you take those particular classes all day long? But no, they make you take all the other annoying classes in a need to make you "well rounded", right? Same thing happens in college.

I was pursuing a science degree but I was forced to take a few humanities classes. SIGH.

The upside to my situation at the time was that Cornell had about a zillion different options of classes I could take. I got to work. I took the course catalog and scanned it in order to find the easiest course. The course that would require very little effort. The course where I would earn an A without having to do any work.

With that mindset, I came across a class called "Meditation in Indian Culture". Awesome. I could totally take a class where we learn about meditation. That just means we sit around with our eyes closed, right? No brainer - that class was for me.

Long story short: I did not get an A.

My professor was an intriguing, Indian man who had a lilting accent and a kind demeanor. He told interesting stories. He had a very relaxed manner to him that permeated the room. Just to be in his presence made you feel calm and content. So there I would sit, a few times a week, trying to get an easy A. In each class, I listened to his stories, absorbed the information...and fell asleep.

Never in my life had I ever fallen asleep in a class before. NEVER. Suddenly, I was nodding off during every class. Curious.

Our homework for this class was to meditate every day and to keep a journal. Well, I lived in the dorms with a roommate who really was not interested in the fact that I needed to sit quietly for 20 minutes every day. As you can imagine, my journal entries were not particularly deep or thoughtful. Mix that together with the fact that I fell asleep and missed information during every class and the result is a non-A student.

This was not a particularly successful venture for me. I did complete the humanities credit and was able to get back to biochemistry, but I didn't get that A for which I had hoped.

Regardless, something about that class stuck with me. Not the meditation practice - I wouldn't come back to that type of mindfulness for another 10 years. It was the professor. There was something about the professor that I just couldn't shake.

I had never met a person who was at peace the way he was. He never seemed stressed. He was immensely kind but held firm to his guidelines, all while smiling and making you feel comfortable. I could not get over the fact that all I had to do was be in the same room as him and I immediately felt calm and at peace too.

He spoke to us about his voice one day. (Luckily, I was awake for this.) He told us that his voice did not used to be calm and rhythmic. He told us that this is a side effect of practicing meditation for many years. Meditation is a practice. You commit to doing it. Over time, all of these pleasant side effects show up. Feeling at peace. Not getting upset as easily. The ability to be kind without letting people walk all over you. Having a calming presence and voice.

As a stressed out, SNS-activated 19-year-old, I couldn't make sense of this. Even though I was wrapped up in the world of science, I had no science that could explain this phenomenon to me. He was trying to tell me that if I sat still every day and focused on my breathing and I did that for several years, suddenly I would have all of these super powers?

In what world does that make sense? How could that possibly occur? How could I even believe this? And also, please please please let it be true. I don't want to feel so stressed out and restless anymore.

This professor and the experience of taking this class has stayed with me through the years. As I said, I would not act on the knowledge until many years later, but he was a constant fixture in my mind. I wanted to feel every day the way that professor made me feel. I did not realize it but it had become a solid goal in the back of my mind.

So Let's Do It Already

Okay. Enough talk. Enough philosophy. Enough of Danielle's rambling stories about chocolate, and boots, and really nice professors. It's time to learn some mindfulness skills.

As mentioned in a past chapter, there are many many many many (you get it) ways to practice mindfulness. All you are doing is giving the mind a job to do so that it will stop creating huge stories that you get caught up in. This chapter will cover the basics of doing this in a seated position.

So. I have to teach you how to sit. But, you know, sit the right way.

How to Sit, You Know, the Right Way

Decide where you would like to sit. You can sit on the floor or in a chair.

If sitting on the floor, you might like to sit on the very edge of a pillow or cushion. Don't sit straight on top of the cushion, just the very edge. This will tilt the pelvis and make you feel way comfortable. Back straight. Chin parallel to the ground.

If sitting in a chair, maneuver yourself so that your feet are flat on the floor. If you are short like me, that means you have to scoot forward in the chair until your feet can solidly touch the floor. Another option is to place books or pillows underneath your feet to make them feel flat on the floor. Back straight. Sit tall, do not lean back into the chair. Chin parallel to the ground.

Relax your hands into a comfortable position. Some people just lay the palms on the thighs. Others like to fold the hands in the lap.

Close the eyes or gaze gently towards the floor or a fixed position.

Seems like a lot of instructions just for sitting. Why do we need all of these? I don't think it will surprise you to say the answer involves science. When we sit for mindfulness, we make sure that the spine is tall. We are not leaning back on anything. We are most definitely not laying down, unless we have certain injuries or medical conditions that require us to do so. The reason for this is that when we are practicing mindfulness we are trying to be very alert, very aware. When we relax the core muscles and slump back in our chairs or lay down, our nervous system sends a signal to the brain saying that we don't need to pay attention. It is time to relax. Perhaps it is time to sleep, like a certain college meditation student in 1999. On the contrary, when we engage the core muscles to sit tall, the nervous system sends the signal that we are alert and paying attention.

Next, think about the hands. Our hands tend to mirror our mood. When we are fidgety, it is hard to keep the hands still. Fidgety hands = fidgety mind. Since we are trying to accomplish the opposite, we focus on relaxing the hands when we sit for mindfulness. You can find any comfortable position for them as long as the hands and arms can feel completely relaxed.

Onto the legs. When we sit, we try to make our body parts as comfortable as we can. Two minutes into our session, we don't want to have achy knees or feet that have already gone to sleep and lost all sensation. When the body becomes uncomfortable, our mind becomes active and it is very hard to pull out of the thoughts. So, when preparing to sit, we put some effort into thinking into the future and trying to prevent as much discomfort as possible. Sitting on the very edge of a cushion will prevent discomfort in our lower backs and knees. When in a chair, sitting with our feet flat to the floor prevents the legs and feet from losing sensation due to constricted blood vessels. If sitting mindfulness becomes a practice you enjoy, you will figure out all the little "rules" for your body and how to sit in the most comfortable, but awake, manner possible.

How about the eyes? Check this out. The eyes are an extension of the brain. Not even lying. Your eyes are a part of the brain that are open to the world. This means that your gaze is directly connected to your brain. Your mind (thoughts) move at the same speed as your gaze. When your gaze is moving all around, flicking from one item to another, taking it all in, your thoughts are also moving all around. On the other hand, when your gaze is still, your thoughts will become still as well. (Try it out. It's pretty cool.)

If I have grossed you out enough about your visible brain parts, then I do believe we are ready to move on.

...And Then???

So we're sitting. Yay. Now what?

Our job in mindfulness, let's remember, is to give the mind (the genie) a job to do so that we can release ourselves from the thoughts. There are many different jobs we can give the mind. We tell the mind to focus on one thing. It can really be any one thing. In general, here are the steps to mindfulness.

Steps to Seated Mindfulness

1. Find a comfortable, seated position.
2. Take a moment to settle in. Come to the present moment. What do you see/hear/feel/smell?
3. Close the eyes or gaze gently towards the floor or a fixed position.
4. Choose one thing to focus on. (More details coming on this!)
5. Allow thoughts to float up, but practice not getting caught in them. You're at the movie theater watching the thoughts float across the screen. Just notice them and then refocus on your one thing.
6. Do step #5 over and over and over again.
7. When you are ready to finish your session, do so slowly. Take a few deep breaths. Stretch the arms and legs. When you are ready, open or refocus the eyes.

The majority of your time in mindfulness will be the middle section. You will focus on one thing. Then, inexplicably, you will suddenly notice that you are caught in your thoughts.

What? When did that happen? Not a problem. Just pull out of the thoughts. Imagine them on the screen at the movie theater. Then, refocus on your one thing.

You will seriously do this so many times that it will feel super annoying. In fact, this is when you will want to quit. At that moment, remind yourself of my amazing college professor and his super powers. He developed them by practicing this over and over for years. The truth is that the more you practice, the longer you can go before you get caught up in those pesky thoughts. Practice may not make perfect, but it will definitely make calm and peaceful.

And Now for a Brief History of Yoga

I interrupt our regularly scheduled programming to bring you a brief history of yoga. Why? Why, you say? To answer, I will tell you to trust me, little cricket, for all shall make sense very soon.

Remember how mindfulness has certain stereotypes in society? Yeah, well yoga has even more. Stereotypes to the tenth power. What do you think of when you hear the word yoga? I bet the images in your head are something along the lines of crazy, bendy poses, clean rooms with soft lighting, and cool leggings (of course). When you think of the type of people who call themselves yogis, you probably think of peaceful people who talk in low voices who have flexible, tall, and skinny bodies and who are ALWAYS happy.

Be prepared for me to shatter your expectations.

I am someone who calls myself a yogi; however, I certainly was not always one. I went to my first yoga class when I was 34. I only went because I suddenly, out of the blue, started having panic attacks and horrible anxiety. All. The. Time. It was terrible. I have never felt so scared in my life. I eventually ended up in therapy and my wonderful, fantastic, superhero of a therapist suggested that I try yoga.

I had so many stereotypes in my head about yoga and yogis that I signed up for a class that took place in a county park. It felt safer than a yoga studio. All those perfect, skinny people bending into pretzely poses with immediate ease? All the soft-spoken humans who had everything figured out and were already perfectly content with life? No way. No no no no way.

So I went to the park, where I was the youngest person in the class. We would walk around the park for 30 minutes and then do some gentle yoga beside picnic tables for another 30 minutes. The ladies in class were loud, hilarious, and honest. We shared stories about our lives...and then we stretched a little. We ended up knowing more about each other than many of our other friends did...and then we breathed a little. It was surprisingly and amazingly fantastic.

The doctors had tried for months to rid me of anxiety and panic, to no avail. A few weeks with these ladies, walking and talking, breathing and bending, and my anxiety was suddenly under control. It was not gone (it will never be gone) but I could see it clearly and I started to manage it.

In my head, though, I did not consider this yoga. We did not do any crazy poses; we did not talk in hushed tones; none of us had anything figured out in our lives. I don't even think any of us wore leggings (whaaattt?). I kept going because it was working and I had started to look forward to my sessions, but in the back of my mind, the little voice wouldn't stop reminding me, "You're not actually doing yoga. You're not actually doing yoga. You're not actually doing yoga."

It took me two years - TWO YEARS - to build up enough courage to go to an actual yoga studio. Even though I enjoyed my park yoga and even though my park yoga teacher taught a class at the local studio, I talked myself out of it for two years. I just couldn't bring myself to go to a place where people had found inner peace and knew how to live life perfectly. I would be an imposter. I had absolutely nothing figured out, except that I liked to walk and talk to the ladies at the park.

I did eventually go, as I'm sure you have deduced by now. And guess what? No one at the studio had ANYTHING figured out in their lives. There were people of all shapes and sizes. Some wore leggings, some wore sweatpants, some wore shorts. Some people laughed out loud during class and some snored during savasana (the relaxing part at the end). Some were indeed super bendy but many were like me (barely bendy at all). The stereotypes did not hold. The common thread, however, was that every person at the yoga studio was determined to be honest about their lives and were actively trying to grow and learn about themselves. They were an extended version of the ladies in the park.

So...I am now someone who calls herself a yogi.

It's a nice story and all, you may be thinking, but why did I feel the need to tell you?

Because.

Because because because...

Yoga originated in India over 5,000 years ago. The purpose of yoga, way back then, was NOT to do bendy poses or to wear leggings or to pretend that you have it all figured out. If you go to India, even today, and say that you are doing yoga, people will think that you mean meditation. The original intent of yoga was meditation, or what we have been calling mindfulness. Meditation was the practice that was known to still the mind and the thoughts so that one could reconnect with the true self hiding in the cave behind the heart. Meditation was known to be the pathway to peace.

As people practiced meditation, they started to realize that it was difficult to sit still for long periods of time. Their knees ached, the back was sore, maybe even the shoulders and neck. So they started to find stretches to do before they sat still in meditation. They discovered that doing some poses built strength in the body and also created flexibility. These two things allowed them to sit still for longer periods of time in order to find inner peace.

As the practice of yoga immigrated to the western world, people filtered out the meditation aspect and just focused on the physical body. Over time, this has created the stereotypes that kept me away from a yoga studio for way longer than necessary.

So the real purpose of yoga is much closer to walking and talking with ladies in a park and then sitting still to breathe than it is to what society would have you think about "yoga".

Which brings us to...

Umm...Focus on What?

Good question. I keep saying you can focus on any one thing during mindfulness. How about the creepy, crawly legs of hairy spiders? Maybe you could focus on the image of a clown in a dark room? The eerie laugh of a psychotic criminal?

Hmm. Perhaps we need some more guidance.

For this guidance, we will look to - and here it is, the moment where things come together - The Yoga Sutras of Patanjali. (Which you would not understand had I not given you the hilarious, introspective, soul-driven commentary about the history of yoga. So, like, I told you that you could trust me. Eye roll.)

Many, many years ago, the wisdom of yoga was passed on via oral tradition. Teachers would instruct one student at a time, passing on all of the stories and knowledge. Eventually, a sage (wise man) named Patanjali decided to collect, organize, and write down all of this information. The result of this endeavor is The Yoga Sutras of Patanjali. This anthology is now seen as a manual for practicing yoga. And to be clear, Patanjali wrote about yoga (meditation) not yoga (bendy poses and perfect people).

In his writings, he gives us more information about what to focus on when we are practicing mindfulness, or as he called it, yoga. Here is his list:

- The inhale and exhale of the breath
- One body part or one of the senses
- The supreme, ever-blissful Light within (I like that one.)
- Any person who you truly admire
- A positive dream you had
- Anything one chooses that is elevating

It is the last item in this list that truly explains all of the rest. People need examples of what to focus on during mindfulness. We need guidance, right? The truth of the matter is that you can focus on ANY one thing. It actually does not matter, as long as that one thing is positive and uplifting. Remember that all we are trying to do is to give the mind one job to do.

When we are in the process of learning, however, this can be overwhelming. If you are given the instruction, "Oh, just focus on one thing. It really doesn't matter what," we will sit there forever trying to figure it out and to make a decision. We will, in fact, think about ALL of the things as we try to decide what ONE thing to think about.

So, Patanjali provides several examples of things people have successfully focused on in the past. These are practices that work for many people. At the very end of the list, after giving examples, he lays the real truth bomb on us that it could literally be anything positive. BUT he provided several literal examples, so we can fall on those until we are confident enough to strike out on our own.

And that, my friend, is a summary of sitting mindfulness. The only thing left to do is to try it for yourself.

To that end, I am providing some additional instructions for how to focus on the breath, on one body part, on sensations, or the supreme, ever-blissful Light within (because it's the most beautiful phrase I have ever read so we should all try to do that one). Take notes as you go. Which methods do you love? Which methods do you detest? And isn't that interesting.

Counting the Breath

In this method, we do not try to control the breath at all, we are just paying attention to it. We will count the breaths as a way to keep our mind focused on it. This is the method that I started with and it really helped me to stay out of my crazy thoughts.

1. Find your comfortable seated mindfulness position.
2. Start to notice the breath.
3. When you feel ready, begin counting each inhale and exhale as you work your way up to the number 10 (or any number you wish).
4. "Inhale 1...exhale 1...inhale 2...exhale 2...inhale 3...exhale 3..."
5. After you count up to the number you have chosen, start to count backwards until you get back down to 1.
6. "Inhale 10...exhale 10...inhale 9...exhale 9...inhale 8...exhale 8..."
7. If you suddenly notice that you have become caught in your thoughts and you have stopped counting, it's ok! Simply start back at number 1 and try again.
8. When you are finished, slowly come out of the mindfulness by moving the body and opening the eyes.

Why Focus on the Breath?

People are always going on and on about focusing on the breath. But why? Why should we focus on the breath? The answer, my friend, involves science. (At this point in the book, does this really surprise you??)

The act of breathing is connected to the sympathetic nervous system (SNS) and the parasympathetic nervous system (PNS). Remember that the SNS is the fight or flight system and the PNS is the rest and digest system. If you spend too much time in SNS activation, you will feel stressed, anxious, and have negative health conditions. If you spend too much time in PNS activation, you might feel low motivation, depression, and have different health conditions.

We can use the breath to help us manage the SNS and PNS. Here's how: Every time we inhale, the SNS is activated. Every time we exhale, the PNS is activated. If you spend more time inhaling, the SNS will be more active than the PNS. On the other hand, if you spend more time exhaling, the PNS will be more active than the SNS.

When we focus on our breath during mindfulness, we can achieve a few different things. If we focus on making the inhales and exhales the same length, then we are bringing balance to the nervous system. This will make us feel calm and stable. If we focus on making the exhales last longer than the inhales, then we are activating the PNS and we will start to feel very calm and relaxed.

Try it!

The Even Breath

The exercise will bring balance to your nervous system. This is great to do if you feel like you are scattered or all over the place and you just want to come back to yourself.

1. Find your comfortable seated mindfulness position.
2. Start to notice the breath.
3. When you feel ready, start counting the lengths of your inhales and exhales. The goal is to make the inhales and exhales last the same amount of time.
4. Count the duration of your inhales: "Inhale 1, 2, 3, 4"
5. Count the duration of your exhales, allowing them to be the same length: "Exhale 1, 2, 3, 4"
6. You decide the number that you count to. I used these numbers as an example.
7. Keep going for the duration of your mindfulness practice. If at any point you feel dizzy or out of breath, stop the counting and come back to your natural breathing.
8. When you are finished, slowly come out of the mindfulness by moving the body and opening the eyes.

The Uneven Breath

The Uneven Breath is one of my favorites! This practice is wonderful to activate the PNS system. So you can do this whenever you need to move away from feeling stressed or too energized and you want to feel more calm and relaxed. This can be used during stressful events but also right before bed so that you can fall asleep quickly.

1. Find your comfortable seated mindfulness position.
2. Start to notice the breath.

3. When you feel ready, start counting the lengths of your inhales and exhales. The goal is to make the exhales last longer than the inhales.
4. Count the duration of your inhales: "Inhale 1, 2, 3, 4"
5. Count the duration of your exhales, allowing them to be longer than the inhales: "Exhale 1, 2, 3, 4, 5, 6"
6. You decide the number that you count to. I used these numbers as an example.
7. Keep going for the duration of your mindfulness practice. If at any point you feel dizzy or out of breath, stop the counting and come back to your natural breathing.
8. When you are finished, slowly come out of the mindfulness by moving the body and opening the eyes.

The Square Breath

This technique involves holding the breath. Some people love this and feel it makes them incredibly calm. Other people really really despise it. Find out for yourself! Do pay attention to how you are feeling. If at any point you feel a little dizzy, that is your sign to stop controlling the breath and just let it rise and fall on its own.

1. Find your comfortable seated mindfulness position.
2. Start to notice the breath.
3. When you feel ready, start counting the lengths of your inhales and exhales. You will also start holding your breath at the top of the inhale and at the bottom of the exhale. You will hold each position (inhale, hold, exhale, hold) for the same amount of time.
4. Count the duration your inhale: "Inhale 1, 2, 3, 4"
5. Hold the breath: "Hold 1, 2, 3, 4"
6. Count the duration of your exhale: "Exhale 1, 2, 3, 4"
7. Hold the breath: "Hold 1, 2, 3, 4"

8. You decide the number that you count to. I used these numbers as an example.
9. Keep going for the duration of your mindfulness practice. If at any point you feel dizzy or out of breath, stop the counting and come back to your natural breathing.
10. When you are finished, slowly come out of the mindfulness by moving the body and opening the eyes.

The 4-7-8 Technique (a/k/a Danielle's Favorite)

This technique is my favorite because it makes me feel SUPER incredibly calm. After breathing like this for 5-10 minutes, my thoughts slow down and I feel amazing. Ridiculously amazing. This technique uses the counts of 4, 7 and 8; however, I count to different numbers each time, depending on how I feel that day. You will use an inhale - hold - exhale pattern. Similar to the Square Breath except that you do not hold your breath after the exhale. The idea to stick to is that the inhale lasts the least amount of time and then you hold the breath and exhale for longer amounts of time.

1. Find your comfortable seated mindfulness position.
2. Start to notice the breath.
3. When you feel ready, start counting the lengths of your inhales and exhales. You will also start holding your breath at the top of the inhale. Follow this pattern: inhale-hold-exhale-inhale-hold-exhale (repeat).
4. Count the duration of your inhale: "Inhale 1, 2, 3, 4"
5. Hold the breath: "Hold 1, 2, 3, 4, 5, 6, 7"
6. Count the duration of your exhale: "Exhale 1, 2, 3, 4, 5, 6, 7, 8"
7. Repeat.
8. You decide the number that you count to. I used these numbers as an example.

9. Keep going for the duration of your mindfulness practice. If at any point you feel dizzy or out of breath, stop the counting and come back to your natural breathing.
10. When you are finished, slowly come out of the mindfulness by moving the body and opening the eyes.

One Body Part

If focusing on the breath makes you feel crazy, then don't do that! There are many other things to focus on. In this exercise, you can practice focusing on just one body part. Intensely. You could choose any body part: tip of the nose, the space between the eyebrows, maybe even the pinky toe.

1. Find your comfortable seated mindfulness position.
2. Start to notice the breath.
3. When you feel ready, bring your focus to the one body part that you have chosen for today. Think solely about this body part. How does it feel? What can it feel? You might wiggle it gently and slowly to see how that feels.
4. Keep going for the duration of your mindfulness practice.
5. When you are finished, slowly come out of the mindfulness by moving the body and opening the eyes.

Sensations

This is another technique you can use if focusing on the breath is not comfortable for you. In this practice, you will simply think about and focus on the sensations that you feel in your body. You can use the senses of hearing, touch, and emotional feeling. We can use sight but know that moving the eyes around sometimes aggravates your thought patterns. If this is the case, remove sight from this practice for yourself.

1. Find your comfortable seated mindfulness position.
2. Start to notice the breath.
3. When you feel ready, start thinking about what your senses are noticing in this specific moment.
4. What do I hear right now? Try to pick up on even the quietest sounds.
5. What do I feel in or on my body? Notice every sensation that you feel (your clothes, the chair, etc.).
6. What do I see around me? What are the colors? Shapes? (Disregard this one if it promotes too much thinking.)
7. What emotions do I feel within myself right now? Can you name them? Where do you feel them in your body?
8. Keep going for the duration of your mindfulness practice.
9. When you are finished, slowly come out of the mindfulness by moving the body and opening the eyes.

The Supreme, Ever-Blissful Light Within

This one is just lovely! Definitely try it at least once and see what you think. This exercise tends to stimulate feelings of love and connection, because it focuses on the area where the heart is located. It makes me feel both calm AND happy.

1. Find your comfortable seated mindfulness position.
2. Start to notice the breath.
3. When you feel ready, start to imagine that there is a shiny ball of light right inside of your chest, in the same location as your heart. With every inhale you take, you can imagine that the ball of light is growing larger. With every exhale you take, you can imagine that the ball becomes its original size again.
4. There is another version of this exercise where you imagine a flower in your chest. With every inhale, you

imagine the petals of the flower are opening. With every exhale, you imagine the petals are folding up again.

5. Keep going for the duration of your mindfulness practice.

6. When you are finished, slowly come out of the mindfulness by moving the body and opening the eyes.

~~LIFE LESSON #8: Whatever you do, don't think about spiders.~~ For real. But, okayyyyy, I'll try again.

LIFE LESSON #8: Sitting mindfulness = Sit + Focus + Refocus + Repeat

SIT +
FOCUS +
REFOCUS +
REPEAT
LIFE LESSON #8

Chapter Summary

- Danielle was not a good meditation student in college. Do not fall asleep in class like she did.
- To sit for mindfulness: sit tall, engage the core, and relax the arms and legs. Close the eyes or find a soft gaze in one direction.
- During sitting mindfulness, focus on any one thing that is positive and uplifting. If you need more guidance than this, here are a few examples of what you can focus on: the breath, one body part, sensations, the Light within, one person you admire, or a positive dream.
- Most of your time spent in mindfulness will be on pulling out of the thoughts. Every time you notice your mind has wandered away from that one area of focus, just gently pull back, pretend you are at the movie theater watching your thoughts, and then refocus on your one thing. Again and again. Over time, you will spend more time NOT caught in the thoughts.
- True yoga refers to meditation (mindfulness). The poses that we now call yoga originated as a way for the body to become stronger and more flexible so that a person could sit still for longer periods of time before becoming uncomfortable.

To Do List

- Create memes showing the difference between the original purpose of yoga versus what society believes about yoga today.
- Choose a different type of sitting mindfulness to do each day. Start with 3 minutes at a time. (We can do anything for 3 minutes, right?)

- Think about the different aspects of science involved with 1) "correct" sitting for mindfulness or 2) focusing on the breath. Create a pamphlet, illustration, or infographic teaching people about this.

8

Mindfulness Whilst Moving

A Story about Math

Oh no, you're thinking. Not math. She already bombarded us with science. All the science. Too much science.

Ha! As if you would be thinking that. We both know there's no such thing as too much science.

But, ya, math. Let's talk about math. Does that make you nervous? Does the mention of math make your SNS spike? Well, let's make a deal. I won't really talk about math, but I will talk about a mathematician.

Let me introduce you to Laurent Schwartz, a French mathematician. Laurent Schwartz made incredible contributions to the theory of distributions. (I don't know what that is. I don't think you know what that is either. Luckily, for this story, it doesn't matter.) In 1950, he was awarded the Fields Medal for his work. That's a big deal. The Fields Medal is the highest honor you can achieve as a mathematician. Whoa. Congrats, Laurent.

Here comes the interesting twist.

When Laurent Schwartz was in high school, he thought he was stupid. His teachers thought he was challenged. He had trouble keeping up. Taking notes was a serious issue. Other students in the class almost always knew the answers to questions before he did. He could eventually determine the answer but it took him a loooooong time to get there.

What Laurent eventually figured out was that he wasn't un-intelligent but he was slow. He was a deep thinker who needed to analyze and think about questions from all angles before he answered. He required a lot more time to come up with answers because he was thinking intensely about them. As we can see from his later accomplishments, this method really worked for him; however, his school at that time evaluated intelligence via how quickly a student could answer a question. According to this system, he was indeed "stupid".

The moral of this story can be summed up by a quotation by Albert Einstein, another mathematician: "Everybody is a genius. But if you judge a fish by its ability to climb a tree, it will live its whole life believing that it is stupid."

Everybody is a genius, but you have to find the correct way to evaluate that.

Everybody is talented, but you have to be open enough to observe it.

Everybody can do mindfulness, but you have to find the method that works.

Do you see how I just slipped that right in there without you noticing? Oh, you did notice? Well. Catching you off guard is not my type of genius.

You would not believe how many people have told me that mindfulness just isn't for them. To all of these people, I say, "Be like Laurent Schwartz." What if mindfulness is for you but you haven't discovered the right method yet? What if you are judging yourself on your mindfulness abilities based on what society deems is correct? What if you do not fit into society's box of what mindfulness is supposed to be? What if you are secretly a mindfulness master? You could totally be a Yoda in disguise but you gave up after trying just one or two types of mindfulness. Oh man, that would be a shame.

As I mentioned before, there is a popular opinion in society and therefore the media that mindfulness means sitting still, closing the eyes, and finding your inner peace. So much so that many people believe that if they try that and hate it, then they are stupid at mindfulness just like Laurent Schwartz thought he was stupid at math.

Well, my friend, I am here to Albert Einstein you. Fishes don't know how to climb trees. We can't judge them on that criteria. Duh. Maybe you are a mindfulness fish and you just can't sit still. That does not mean mindfulness is not for you. It just means you shouldn't do mindfulness while sitting still. Double duh. Duh cubed. Duh = mc². That's what this chapter is about. It's about Laurent Schwartz discovering he was a genius and it's about you discovering you are a mindfulness fish (you know, metaphorically). It's about breaking out of the box of what mindfulness is supposed to be and remembering that mindfulness can be anything as long as you stick to its original purpose.

You get to decide what mindfulness works for you. I happen to be a Sitting Mindfulness Genius. All of the methods discussed in the last chapter? Ya, those are my jam. Although, now that I think about it, I don't follow any of the breathing exercises exactly as I wrote them. I took parts of one exercise and merged them with another until I created the truly perfect method for me.

This chapter is giving you permission to try some different methods. You are your own scientist. You will experiment with lots of different practices, take some data, and figure out what type of Mindfulness Genius you are.

The Genie Rule

Here's the one rule to keep in mind as we start exploring the mindfulness realm of possibilities. I said above that anything can be mindfulness as long as you stick to its original purpose.

The original purpose of mindfulness: Stop letting the thoughts control you. Stop getting caught up in the stories the thoughts try to tell us. To do this, we give the mind a job to do. One thing to focus on.

The Genie Rule of Mindfulness: Give the mind one positive thing to focus on. One very specific thing.

That's it. Other than that, there are infinite possibilities.

You could garden and, while doing so, focus solely on the way the soil feels in your fingers.

You could doodle and, while doing so, focus solely on the very subtle sound the colored pencil makes as you move it across the page.

You could sweep the floor and, while doing so, focus solely on the repetitive motion of the broom.

You could even eat dark chocolate and, while doing so, focus solely on the taste of the chocolate.

Infinite possibilities.

Anything is mindfulness as long as you are giving the genie a job to do. (Otherwise, if you remember, he will destroy you. dum Dum DUM)

The Collecting of the Data

Science. Again. I know...

Here's the thing. You're a Mindfulness Genius but you don't know it yet. You need to figure out your special mindfulness thing. Does sitting still make you feel calm and peaceful and super amazing? Maybe it makes you feel crazy and anxious. Ok. That's helpful information.

If we're going to figure out your particular type of genius, we need to be organized. We need to think like a scientist. We need to collect data. DATA. Can you feel how excited I am? Cause I am. Excited, that is.

Don't worry. This is easy. I'm going to walk you through it step-by-step.

To know if a mindfulness method is working for you (or terrifically not), we need to know how you feel before you start compared to how you feel after you try it. For example, if you feel caught up in the thoughts before you do mindfulness and then you still feel that way afterwards, maybe that method does not work for you. Or...maybe you can't necessarily blame that on the mindfulness. It's possible that's just you for today! BUT. If you are caught up in the thoughts before you start and afterwards you feel incredibly peaceful and present, then we've found one of your mindfulness methods.

To know this info, we need to write it down in an organized way. Which can only mean one thing. Oh yes. DATA TABLE. This chapter keeps getting better and better.

Collecting Mindfulness Data

1. Write down today's date and the time in the table.
2. Choose which mindfulness method you would like to try. Write this in the table.
3. Before you start, write down two numbers. Rate yourself on a scale of 1 to 5 on how calm you are and how focused you are. 5 would mean super duper calm or crazy amazingly focused. 1 would mean you forget what the

word calm means or you can't remember what you are reading right now.

4. Complete the mindfulness technique you have chosen.
5. Afterwards, rate yourself again. On a scale of 1 to 5, how calm are you and how focused are you? Write this down.

Date/ Time	Before: Calm	Before: Focus	Type of Mindfulness (What did you focus on?)	After: Calm	After: Focus

The Analyzing of the Data

We've got data. We've got a data table. We've got data written down in a data table.

So now what?

Now, my friend, let's look at the data. What patterns do you observe?

Here are some things to notice:

- Look for any techniques where you noticed an improvement in calm or focus afterwards.
- Notice if there are some techniques that result in you being more calm but not more focused. This is useful for those times when what you really want is to calm down.

- Notice if there are some techniques that result in you being more focused but not more calm. This is useful for those times when what you really want is to focus on a task.
- Are there any techniques where you felt less calm and less focused afterwards? I suggest trying that technique one more time just to verify, but you may have found something that is not for you.
- Does the time of day matter? Does it form a pattern? For example, every time you do mindfulness in the morning, do you like it? When you do mindfulness at night, do you fall asleep? The time of day can tell you something about when mindfulness has optimal results for you.

Isn't this the coolest thing ever? By writing down some information, you are narrowing the search for your particular Mindfulness Genius.

Now that you are ready to be a data collecting machine, here are some step-by-step techniques that do not involve sitting still. These are just some ideas. Remember, you have permission to try anything as long as you stick to the Rule of the Genie.

Walking Mindfulness

1. Find an empty, quiet place to walk. It does not have to be a huge space. Even just the length of a yoga mat can work for this.
2. Your purpose in this mindfulness is to focus solely on what your feet feel as they walk. Stand at one end of your space and very slowly place one foot in front. Start to walk towards the other end of the space.
   - What do the soles of your feet feel?

- Can you feel the weight slowly changing from the heel to the ball of the foot?
- Can you feel your toes flex as you push off one foot onto another?
- What else can you notice?

3. If you are wondering if you are going slowly enough, you are not. Walk slower. Even slower. EVEN SLOW-ER THAN THAT.

4. If you get caught up in your thoughts and stop thinking about your feet, just notice that and refocus on your feet.

5. When you are finished, take a deep breath, smile, and enjoy your day.

Eating Mindfulness

1. Choose one thing to eat. It could be anything. Common items are: an orange, a raisin, a cookie, or a piece of chocolate.

2. Notice how it feels in your hand. Is there a texture?

3. Hold it up to your nose. Is there a smell?

4. Place a small piece in your mouth (or take a small bite). What does the texture feel like in your mouth? What are the first flavors that you notice?

5. Let it sit in the mouth for a moment. Do the flavors change? Does the texture change as you chew or as it melts in the mouth?

6. Eat slowly. Even slower. Ya, even slower than that.

7. Continue on in this manner until you have eaten the entire food item. If you get caught in the thoughts, simply notice that and refocus on the food.

8. When you are finished, take a deep breath, smile, and enjoy your day.

Coloring/Doodling

1. Choose a coloring page or decide if you would like to simply doodle. Collect your pens, colored pencils, markers, or any other supplies.
2. Start to color or doodle. As you do, focus on one aspect of the coloring. Perhaps the feel of the pencil on the paper. Could be the sound of the pencil. Perhaps focus on the sight of the colors or doodles. Put all of your awareness on this one thing.
3. Take your time. There is no hurry. There is no deadline. There is no required finished product.
4. When you are finished, take a deep breath, smile, and enjoy your day.

Movement & Breath

1. In this technique, you will combine movement and breathing. It can be any movement. Seriously. The movement should ideally have at least two parts, such as raising your arms and lowering your arms. (This is the example we will use.)
2. For one part of the movement, inhale. Example: As you raise your arms, inhale.
3. For the second part of the movement, exhale. Example: As you lower your arms, exhale.
4. Move slowly so that your breaths are long and easeful.
5. Repeat over and over and over again.
6. When you have finished, sit/stand without movement and relax your breath for a minute or two. Then, smile and enjoy your day.

P.S. You really can use any movement for this. I once had a student who experienced anxiety during tests. She would sit at her desk and place her palm on the surface. Then, she would raise one finger up and lower it down as she breathed. This calmed her enough to then take her test.

P.P.S. This is why people find yoga poses calming. Many yoga classes are taught in a manner where the teacher is telling you when to inhale and when to exhale. By the end of the class, you have coordinated your movement and breath for a long period of time. Boom - mindfulness!

Music

1. Choose a song to listen to for this technique. It should be instrumental (just music, no words). When we hear words, our brain engages and we are trying to disengage our brains!
2. Close your eyes or rest the eyes gently in one place.
3. Start listening to the song.
4. Focus solely on the sound. What do you notice? What does it sound like?
5. Do you feel any emotions from the music? Where in your body do you feel it?
6. If you get caught in the thoughts, just notice this and refocus on the sound.
7. At the end of the song, take a deep breath, smile, and enjoy your day.

Starting with one song is a great way to try this technique. If you enjoy this type of mindfulness, you will slowly be able to listen for longer amounts of time, eventually building an entire playlist that you can listen to.

~~LIFE LESSON #9: Fish can't climb trees so let Einstein do it.~~
What the... That doesn't even make sense.
LIFE LESSON #9: Anything can be mindfulness.

The Really Important Disclaimer

Mindfulness is not magic. It does not miraculously make all your issues and problems disappear. Mindfulness is not a substitute for other tools and interventions that would be beneficial to your mental health.

When I was working through my anxiety and panic attacks, I used a combination of talk therapy, yoga, and mindfulness. That was the "magic" mixture of tools for me.

There are an incredible variety of methods that can be helpful in working through difficult issues. Just to name a few: somatic experiencing, EFT tapping, Reiki, yoga, mindfulness, craniosacral therapy, talk therapy, and medication.

The great thing about mindfulness is that it complements any other methods that you are currently using or thinking about using. Find the right combination for you.

Chapter Summary

- Everyone is a unique type of genius but you have to know how to evaluate it. If you tell a fish to climb a tree, you will end up thinking the fish is stupid. Not only that, but the fish will think it is stupid, too. Along these same lines, mindfulness is for everyone but you have to find the method that matches your type of genius. You have to find your Mindfulness Genius.
- Mindfulness can happen anywhere and in any way as long as you stick to its original purpose. The original purpose of mindfulness: Stop letting the thoughts control you. Stop getting caught up in the stories the thoughts try to tell us.
- To create a mindfulness technique, follow The Genie Rule of Mindfulness: Give the mind one thing to focus on. One very specific thing.
- In order to determine your Mindfulness Genius, start collecting some data. Compare how you feel before you do mindfulness and after you do mindfulness. How does your level of calm compare? How does your level of focus compare? Use Danielle's Superior Data Table of Mindfulness to help you track this information and to find patterns.
- Try lots of techniques + Collect lots of data = Discover your Mindfulness Genius

To Do List

- How does the story of Laurent Schwartz make you feel? Can you relate to it? Do you feel like you are ever evaluated in a way that does not truly measure your supreme abilities? Tell your story! Write it out, draw it, or call a friend and tell them.

- Find a Very Special Notebook that you can use as a mindfulness journal. Use this journal to collect your data about mindfulness techniques.
- Try lots of different mindfulness techniques and collect data on them.
- Make up your own, unique mindfulness technique. Combine a few methods listed in this book or think of something completely different.
- Be you, you beautiful Mindfulness Fish.

Part III

In which I admit that sometimes mindfulness is just the worst.

9

Too. Many. Thoughts.

Don't Do It

I would like to tell you a story. Yes, another one. I just need to ask you for a favor first. While I am telling you this story, please try to focus on it. Whatever you do, DO NOT think about a white rhinoceros. Don't picture it in your mind. Don't think about the words. Nothing about a white rhinoceros. Okay, thanks so much.

When I was taking that meditation class in college, I had mentioned to you that our homework was to meditate every day and to keep a journal about our experiences. (Please stop thinking about the white rhinoceros.) I had a really hard time doing my homework. I lived with a roommate in the college dorms. Do you know what it's like living in the dorms???

First of all, for some reason, the hallway often smelled like fish. It was super gross. There was a student on our floor who microwaved fish a few times a week. The stench was unbelievable. So there's that. (Don't even try to spell rhinoceros.)

Secondly, the noise. 24 hours a day. Not always LOUD but always there. Girls screaming (I think they were laughing but it sounded like screaming); heavy footsteps running down the hall; doors slamming; an odd mixture of different types of music coming from each room. And there I was, sitting on the floor, eyes closed, trying to meditate. (Get that rhinoceros out of your mind.)

All I could think about was how I wasn't able to stop thinking! There were too many things for my mind to grab hold of. (Go away, white rhino.) Mostly, I just ended up feeling angry and frustrated, because my meditations were ridiculously unsuccessful.

Or so I thought.

Let's talk about it.

Did you think about the white rhino???

Did You Do It?

Did you think about the white rhinoceros? Seriously? I only asked you to do one thing. You had one job - to NOT think about the white rhino. You thought about it anyway, didn't you? Hmph.

Remember the genie who destroys you if you don't give it a job to do? (A/k/a our mind) Ya. The genie (our mind) only listens to direct orders of what he should do. He really doesn't listen if you tell him to NOT do something. In fact, when you tell him to stop doing something, he will just do it more.

Case in point: the white rhinoceros.

Says the genie: "Don't think about the white rhinoceros? Ha! Now it will be the only thing you think about!"

Remember, give the genie a job to do; otherwise, he will destroy you.

Going back to my college self who thought she was disastrously horrible at meditation, there I was, sitting in my dorm room, trying to meditate. All the smells and sounds everywhere. I sat and told myself, "Stop thinking about the smell. Don't pay attention to the sounds." So guess what happened? The white rhino happened. I sat there and became consumed with the smell and the sounds.

Sometimes, mindfulness feels horrible. Sometimes, it makes us feel less focused and very NOT calm. Sometimes, I feel worse after mindfulness than before I started.

All of the time, this is okay.

True Confessions of an Aquarium Intern

I'm going to tell you something. Something embarrassing. Something that I feel a bit ashamed about. Something that I don't ever want my kids to know that I did. (Do you think they're reading this right now? Probably not, right? I mean, what kid wants to read a book their mom wrote?)

When I was in college, I was majoring in biology but specifically in marine science. I wanted to be a marine biologist. To that end, one summer I got an internship at an aquarium. Yay for me! It was all happening! This was the first step in a long line of successful jobs that would lead me to save the whales, turtles, and even the weird sea cucumber thingies.

Here's the thing.

This is the thing that no one tells you.

No one wants excited college students to know this thing.

Internships are the worst. So boring. They give you the jobs to do that literally no one else at the business wants to do. Like standing next to the touch tank and requesting that the child NOT climb inside the tank to hug the horseshoe crabs. Or introducing the movie in the movie theater and then sitting there watching the same video over and over again. Or answering the weirdest questions from the visitors. (One guy asked me how we trained the fish not to pee in the tanks. I didn't even know what to say.)

It was a challenging, unpleasant job that had nothing to do with saving the whales, turtles, or even sea cucumbers. It was boring but also stressful. I smelled like fish water all summer. Perhaps, you are saying, I did this with a smile on my face, acting like the professional that I aspired to be one day. Maybe I embraced the experience, learning as much as I could about how to work with the public and teach them about marine animals. It's possible that I found my place in this job, realizing that even the small jobs can have big impacts in the long run.

Or maybe, and here's another idea, just hear me out...maybe I hid under the desks in the back office to avoid my boss who wanted me to do all of those boring things.

Literally.

My fellow intern and I literally hid underneath the desks in the back office to avoid having to talk to the ridiculous visitors. We could hear the footsteps of the people coming to look for us and we would crawl under the desks and remain stationary and silent as they walked through the office calling out our names.

We wouldn't even take a breath until we heard them walking out again, shaking their heads as they mumbled, "Where did those girls get to now?"

Please don't tell my kids.

I was in an unpleasant situation and I chose to hide from it.

In fact, this is just between us. Don't tell anyone.

I did not like what was being asked of me, so I ran away.

Above all else, please, pretty pretty please, do not tell Oprah.

We learned in the first chapter that it is ineffective to try to run away from problems or unfortunate (fortunate?) situations. Regardless of this truth, we tend to run away or try to hide often. All the time. More than you know.

We even do it with our thoughts. Suppose there is a thought in your head that is very true. Your mind is trying to provide you with useful information for your life.

"You are eating too much chocolate."

Guess what I'm going to do with that thought?

I'm going to run away, hide under the desk, and wait for the thought to go away.

How do I do this? How do I hide from my thoughts? Easy. I cover it up with a zillion other thoughts. Any will do. I create a story that is much preferable to the actual thought.

"I read the other day that chocolate contains amazing antioxidants. In fact, I can almost feel them working when I eat chocolate. My students will even tell you that, when I am eating chocolate, I am more upbeat and positive. I gave up chocolate last month and I was a grumpy mess. Eating chocolate is making me a better teacher."

Ya....that thought is way more believable. So plausible. I can feel the antioxidants in my bloodstream right now.

When I was having panic attacks, I later learned that I was hiding from my anxious thoughts. I had anxiety about situations but instead of allowing myself to face those thoughts, I covered them up. I ran away. I kept so busy that there was no time or space for my mind to create any thoughts about anxiety.

When I started doing yoga with the ladies at the park and I realized it was helping, I remembered that old college class I took. I decided it was time to brush off those meditation skills.

Guess what?

Every time I sat still and tried to still the mind, I felt so incredibly anxious I thought I would explode. I could barely stand to close my eyes. The moment I did, I could feel a scream building in my throat and the panic rising behind my eyes. Thirty seconds, maybe one minute. That's all I could handle before I felt like crawling out of my skin.

This sucks! I thought. I hate mindfulness.

Mindfulness was making my thoughts worse.

In actuality, mindfulness was not making my thoughts worse, it was just making me aware of the thoughts. I had spent so many years hiding from my thoughts. The moment I sat still, all of them became visible.

And there were a lot of them.

Mindfulness does not give you more thoughts. Mindfulness makes you aware of the thoughts that are already there.

It took me many practice sessions of sitting still and facing all of the thoughts that I had run away from before mindfulness began to feel peaceful for me.

But How?

How do you face the thoughts that we have run away from for so long? How do we handle a thought that brings us shame, or anger, or anxiety?

Well, let's understand how not to do it and then we can shed some light on the opposite. When I was having anxious thoughts, I ignored them. I did not pay any attention to them. I hid from them under the desk in the back office. Every time an unpleasant thought popped up, I found a different activity to do. Maybe it was time to bake cookies. I should go play with the kids. Definitely need to take the dogs for a walk. You know what would be fun right now? Watching a movie or reading a book. Unintentionally, I gave the genie in my head many, many mindless jobs to do so that I would not have the ability to notice the other thoughts.

I ignored them.

I did not pay attention to them.

I hid from them.

This is helpful information! If I want to stop hiding from thoughts, then I need to do the opposite of what I was doing.

When I became serious about dealing with my anxiety, I used mindfulness to help me stop hiding. I would sit still, focus on my breath, and allow those thoughts to occur. I paid attention to them. I gave them permission to be present. I acknowledged them.

"I don't want my husband to travel for work. It makes me scared to take care of the children with no one to help me."

This is a true statement. I was scared to be a solo parent.

The first time I allowed this thought to pop up, I was so surprised. I actually had no idea that I was scared about this. I knew I didn't like it when he traveled but I had been dealing with it through anger! Turns out I wasn't angry. Nope. Not angry. I was scared witless.

Wow.

I'm scared.

Okay.

So I sat there, for only a few minutes each day (because that's all I could handle at the beginning), I focused on my breath, and

I allowed all of the scary thoughts to surface. I paid attention to all of them. Just for a few minutes, I allowed them to exist. Then, I got up and went about my day.

I didn't say the thoughts were bad. I didn't say the thoughts were good. I paid attention to the thoughts and said, "Well, isn't that interesting."

That's all.

You will most certainly have more thoughts when you begin a mindfulness practice. Let them be there. Some of them will be hilarious. ("I wonder what would happen if I threw a cupcake at Bree's face?") Some will be weird. ("If a platypus mated with a porcupine, what would their babies look like?") Some will be difficult. ("I'm scared that I'm not a good mom.") Some will be downright inappropriate. ("You're eating too much chocolate.")

When you have too many thoughts, you're not bad at mindfulness. You're actually very successful at mindfulness. Focus on your one thing and allow the thoughts to exist. When you allow something to be present, like the white rhino, it stops making you feel crazy.

Who knew? Allowing myself to think anxious thoughts was the cure for my anxious thoughts.

Remember: the thoughts are allowed to be there. The thoughts are not you. You are just watching them. Not good, not bad. Just interesting.

And, to be clear, I'm not eating too much chocolate.

~~LIFE LESSON #10: Internships are so much fun.~~
Hmph.
LIFE LESSON #10: It's time to stop hiding.

Chapter Summary:

- When we tell the mind not to do something, it will try very hard to do that thing. When practicing mindfulness, tell the mind what you want it to do. Do not tell it what you do not want it to do.
- It is a natural tendency for humans to hide from unpleasant situations. This includes our thoughts. We hide from our thoughts by creating stories that are more favorable or by staying busy so that we can't pay attention to the thoughts.
- Experiencing many thoughts while practicing mindfulness is normal. You are not doing anything "wrong". You are not "bad" at mindfulness. You are simply more aware of the thoughts that you are having.
- Use mindfulness to stop hiding from your thoughts. Focus on your one thing, and allow all thoughts to be present. Pay attention to them without judging them or getting caught in them. Think to yourself, "Well, isn't that interesting."

To Do List:

- Eat more chocolate.
- Keep practicing mindfulness techniques. Continue working to find your Mindfulness Genius. On days when the thoughts are too much, pay attention to them. Focus on your mindfulness thing and pay attention.
- Think of a story or scenario where someone hides instead of facing an issue. Choose one of the following:
    - Write a screenplay.
    - Write a letter from the person's future self telling them to stop hiding.
    - Draw a comic strip version of the story.

- Record a news story relaying the story and the moral of the story.

10

Too. Many. Emotions.

I Don't Want to Feel This Much

For real. When I am going through a hard time, the idea of mindfulness makes me want to cry. When I sit still and move out of my thoughts, the emotions that float to the surface are so large. Uncomfortably intense.

I don't want to feel them. I would much rather hide from them.

Oh yes, my friend, we hide from our emotions just as much as we hide from our thoughts.

Why would I ever want to purposefully put myself in a situation that makes me feel worse? Why would I ever do mindfulness if it is going to make these emotions ridiculously present? I want the emotions to go away, not to become bigger.

This is a common complaint when someone is first trying out mindfulness. Sometimes, they might be feeling, you know, generally alright. Then they sit down to practice mindfulness and these large emotions loom up and take over.

No thank you, they say. I was doing just fine before. Only slightly off. Just a bit unhappy. Ok, I admit. I was wildly grumpy and unsatisfied with life. But mindfulness made it worse. There's no way I'm going to continue doing that.

Yeah. I hear you. I've been there and I agree.

Sometimes, mindfulness feels awful.

Let's all quit and go buy some new boots.

Or possibly, perhaps, just maybe, keep reading.

A Short Story

And now, a short story:

There was a man who went to visit his brother. He stayed in a spare bedroom in his brother's house during his visit. On the first night staying in this room, he awoke in the darkness, looked at the ground beside his bed, and saw a snake. The snake was coiled up and preparing to strike. The man reacted immediately, screaming out in fear at the top of his lungs.

The man's brother heard his scream and ran into the bedroom.

"There's a snake about to attack me!" yelled the man.

Alarmed, the brother turned on the light and rushed into the room to help.

As the man and his brother looked for the snake, they both realized that it had been a coil of rope the entire time.

Everything was fine and there was no need to panic at all.

The End.

Umm...Okay

You may be wondering if that story was really necessary.

Maybe.

Let's see, shall we?

The man awoke in the darkness of night and saw a snake on the floor. A snake that most probably was poisonous. A snake that was coiled up and ready to strike. A snake that would kill him if it attacked. The man's nervous system immediately shot into SNS mode, fight or flight. The blood vessels constricted; heart rate skyrocketed; pupils dilated.

Except it wasn't a snake. It was just a rope. There was no need to panic at all.

Here's my question: Does it matter what it was? At that moment in time, does it matter that it was actually a rope?

The truth, in that moment of time, did not matter at all. All that mattered to the man was what his senses were telling him. His sense of sight and thought created information in his brain that it was a snake about to kill him. At that moment, that was the truth to him. His body reacted according to his truth.

This occurs often in our lives. We react to situations, regardless of what the reality is. The truth does not matter to our nervous systems. All that matters is the truth that the senses create in our minds. If the mind declares something a snake, the systems of our bodies will react accordingly.

Do you remember 20-year-old Danielle who was standing at the helm of the sailing vessel, valiantly manning her position and courageously steering through the storm? Her sense of thought told her she was useless and stupid. Her senses said it was all her fault. It does not matter that the truth was very far from this. Her body reacted as if she had done something wrong. Her body reacted in the same way as if she were legitimately experiencing shame and guilt. From that point on, every time someone was needed to steer the sailing vessel, Danielle's SNS spiked and prepared her to either fight or run away, regardless of the reality that she was actually very talented at steering.

Reality does not affect our nervous systems. The story we tell ourselves does.

The emotions we feel can be very large. They are convincing. Just as we have way more thoughts than we are aware of, the same is true of our emotions. It is so very easy to get caught up in our thoughts and, likewise, we can get caught up in the emotions that these thoughts create. The thoughts create emotions, but the emotions lead to larger, more extensive thoughts, which then lead to bigger, overwhelming emotions, and on and on.

It's a bummer, for sure.

Let's work our way out of this pattern.

Break the Cycle

The only way to stop this unhelpful cycle is to interrupt it. This is what we do with mindfulness. In the last chapter, we practiced focusing on one thing and allowing the thoughts to exist. We paid attention to the thoughts. We can do the same thing with emotions.

The man and the brother in our story panicked about the snake until they paused to look at it. Then, they realized everything was fine. It was not a snake at all. Just a rope.

They paused and thereby saw the truth. They paused. There is magic in the pause.

In mindfulness, this is what we are doing. We are creating a pause. We focus the mind on one thing and allow the thoughts. Then, to add one more step to this process, we allow the emotions as well. We pay attention to the emotions. By allowing everything to be there and not being caught up in it, we are creating a pause.

In this pause, we can be aware of what we are feeling. We can name that feeling. And then we can ask it, "Are you a snake or a rope?"

As an example, when I was having panic attacks, I thought that I was so angry at my husband for traveling. It was all his fault and I was losing my mind because of it. When I started to sit still, I realized that the anger was a snake. It wasn't really true. The emotion that floated up during my mindfulness was not anger at all. It was fear. Intense fear. Fear that had grown larger and larger because I had been trying to ignore it. Just like the white rhino, what we ignore grows larger until we pay attention to it.

So, yes. Sometimes, mindfulness does not feel good. Sometimes, things we had no idea we were thinking or feeling appear in front of us in a very large and uncomfortable way. Mindfulness is not magic, but if mindfulness were magic, this is the magic: what you pay attention to in mindfulness will stop haunting your subconscious thoughts and feelings. Once you pay attention to the white rhino, she is very happy to sit at the edge of your mind. She won't interrupt you again.

Let's Be Practical

That sounds really great. In fact, it sounds easy. I'm being haunted by huge, uncomfortable feelings. I think I'll just sit down and pay attention to them and then they'll just - poof! - disappear.

Yeah, I mean, it's true.

But...doesn't feel good. Not as easy as it sounds.

How about a few concrete, practical techniques to use when things feel too big and mindfulness seriously sucks?

Name It

We can do this technique with thoughts and feelings, both positive and negative ones.

1. Settle into your mindfulness practice. Just focus on your one thing for the first few minutes.
2. Allow the thoughts and feelings to float to the surface.
3. Name the thoughts and feelings. Fear, jealousy, anger, resentment, guilt, gratitude, joy, contentment. You can even say, "This is ___. This is how I experience ___."

4. Allow the thought/feeling to be present and then watch as they shift. Sometimes they just fade away, other times they move over to the side as new thoughts/feelings arrive. Like clouds in the sky, watch them form, shift, and then move on.

Invite It In

I'm telling you right now that you are going to read this and slam the book shut. You are going to say, "She's gone too far. It's too weird. I'm out!" Hopefully, you will sneak back and secretly try it, because it works. Have I ever steered you wrong yet? No, no I haven't. Trust me.

1. Settle into your mindfulness practice. Just focus on your one thing for the first few minutes.
2. Allow the thoughts and feelings to float to the surface.
3. Name the thoughts and feelings.
4. Then, invite them in as if they are knocking at your front door. You have opened the door and are inviting them in for a dinner party. "Oh, hello, fear. So nice of you to stop by. Please come in." "Anger - how long has it been?! Please, do come sit at the table with me." "Joy! You know you are always welcome here. Come in, come in, I have been waiting to see you."
5. Imagine that you are indeed sitting at a large dinner table with all of your thoughts and feelings there as well.
6. Continue your mindfulness practice, just staying aware of your dinner guests but not interacting with them. Just let them eat dinner in silence.

I'm not even kidding you. It works.

Feel It in the Body

If you are not used to tuning into your body, this one can take some practice. Our bodies and emotions/thoughts are linked together. Think about it: when you are stressed or anxious, you feel it as heartburn, upset stomach, or tense shoulder muscles. Every emotion can create physical sensations in the body. It takes practice to tune into the body, but the results can be very helpful. You can do this practice with both positive and negative thoughts and feelings.

1. Settle into your mindfulness practice. Just focus on your one thing for the first few minutes.
2. Allow the thoughts and feelings to float to the surface.
3. For each thought or feeling, try to locate it in your body. For example, when I feel panicky, I can feel it in my ribcage. The muscles in the ribcage become achy. When I am sad, my shoulders slump over. When I am angry, my entire back clenches up.
4. After you locate the body part that is experiencing the emotion, start to move that body part. In any way. Wave the arms over your head. Do some cat/cow movements with your torso. Bend from side to side. As you move the body, you are moving the emotion. This is a wonderful "trick". Since the emotions affect the body, the opposite can also be true: the body can affect the emotions!

*Remember: we are not trying to get rid of the emotion but we are trying to be very aware of it. By being aware, we are able to shift it.

Know Your Limits

There will be times when the thought or the feeling is a little too overwhelming. At any point, if it feels too large, that is your indication to walk away for that day. I told you that when I first tried mindfulness after having panic attacks, that I could only handle a minute or so at a time. Then, it felt like way too much for me to handle, and I walked away.

If you are practicing mindfulness and something pops up that feels uncomfortable, please use any of the techniques listed above. If something pops up, however, and it is supremely overwhelming and feels like too much, please walk away. At these times, find a physical activity that will place you in the present moment:

- going for a walk or bike ride
- baking or cooking
- playing sports with friends
- any activity where your body is active and you are focused on the task at hand

This is not a form of hiding. This is you and the emotion agreeing that you see each other but that you need to reschedule the meeting for a time that will work better for you.

By sitting with the emotion, even for one minute, you are paying attention to it. Over time, you will be able to sit longer and pay attention more. The overwhelm will begin to fade and then the good stuff starts to happen, especially if you are combining mindfulness with other types of healing tools.

They're Right

So, yeah, all of the skeptics are right. They tried mindfulness but it made them feel worse, not better. This is true. This definitely happens sometimes. I admit to being metaphorically kicked in the butt by mindfulness.

But they're only half right. They don't know the full story. They left during the part of the story where the heroes are down for the count and everything looks dire. They didn't make it to the heroic rescue and the happily ever after.

That's what I'm here to tell you about. Remember my ultra calm and cool meditation professor? The lilting voice, the calm but firm attitude, the ability to make those around him feel peaceful? That's what is waiting for you on the other side of this struggle.

Find your Mindfulness Genie. Allow the thoughts and feelings. Back out if it becomes overwhelming. But always come back the next day, even just for a minute. Always come back. The next day and then the next.

It's worth it. Remember that I've never steered you wrong. Trust me.

LIFE LESSON #11: Danielle went an entire chapter without mentioning chocolate.

Impressive, though not a life lesson at all.

LIFE LESSON #11: Pay attention. (Is it a snake or a rope?)

Chapter Summary

- Sometimes, mindfulness does not feel good because the moment we tune in, large emotions appear. This can be uncomfortable or even overwhelming.
- Our nervous systems react to the stories we tell, not to the actual reality of a situation. We will have thoughts and emotions in response to these stories. If you think you see a snake, you will react as if it is a snake (even if it's just a rope).
- In order to discern what is a snake and what is a rope, we need to pause and see reality. Mindfulness gives us a method to pause so that we can see our thoughts and emotions clearly.
- During mindfulness, focus on your one thing and allow the thoughts and feelings to be present. If you try not to think about them, it will be all you think about!
- To work with emotions when they surface, you can name them, invite them in, or feel them in the body.
- At any point, if an emotion becomes too overwhelming during mindfulness, walk away and engage in a physical task. Then, try again the next day, if only for a minute or so.
- When you show up and pay attention to the uncomfortable emotions, the intensity of the emotions will start to fade. With enough time, you can coexist with the emotions and there is enough room for calm and peace to be present.
- This totally works. Trust Danielle.

To Do List

- What is a big emotion that you would rather not have to feel or deal with? Pay attention to it on purpose. What color would this emotion be? What type of flower or animal would it look like? Where can you feel it in your body? Draw a picture that depicts how this emotion feels to you.

- What is a big emotion that you would really really like to feel more often? Pay attention to it on purpose. What color would this emotion be? What type of flower or animal would it look like? Where can you feel it in your body? Draw a picture that depicts how this emotion feels to you.
- Keep practicing mindfulness techniques. Continue working to find your Mindfulness Genius. On days when the thoughts or feelings are too much, pay attention to them. Focus on your mindfulness thing and pay attention. Use the techniques in this chapter to help you work with them.

11

Superpowers

Remembering

When I was little, my grandpa was my favorite person in the whole wide world. He was always warm, always laughing, always ready for an adventure. Sometimes he would laugh so hard that he would start crying. I was in awe of this ability. I had never seen anyone else in my life who could feel so happy but their body could not contain the happiness so it leaked out of their eyes. Not only that, but when he laughed, his whole body shook. His entire body laughed along with him. His hugs were soft but strong. He would crawl on the ground with my sisters and me, play mini-golf with us, and buy lots and lots of ice cream. He was a wonder.

From an early age, I liked to write poems. Grandpa always had time to read them. Inexplicably, he thought every single poem I wrote was worthy of intense admiration and applause. And I'm telling you, like, they weren't.

He liked to write poems too and he would share his with me and ask my advice about what to write next. It was like we were in a secret club, just Grandpa and me. There was no hiding from Grandpa. He saw me exactly as I was. He saw the true self hiding in the cave behind my heart, even when I started to grow up and could not see it for myself anymore.

At some point, writing poems wasn't really cool, so I stopped. I continued to write to Grandpa, who lived in Canada while I lived in Florida. We would talk on the phone, write letters, and visit once or twice throughout the year. He started telling me that he could not wait to read the book I was going to write one day. In high school, wanting to make him proud, I sat down and tried to write a few books. And that's all I'm going to say about that odd endeavor.

One summer, my grandma started giving me suggestions of what I should write about for a book but Grandpa interrupted her and said, "She's not ready to write that book yet! She's just in high school. She hasn't had enough experiences. She doesn't know anything about life yet."

Yeah, that's right, I thought. It's totally not time yet. Lots of other things to do first. And so writing a book slowly fell into the cave with my true self, forgotten.

Fast forward to a zillion years later, and you will find me in Canada as an adult, attending a family member's funeral. Meanwhile, I was also visiting with Grandpa who was not in fantastic condition.

"Prepare yourself to see him. He is not doing well."

"This will probably be the last time you see him, so enjoy your time with him."

No pressure.

Grandpa was having some memory issues. He couldn't remember people's names. It took him a while to place who you were, even after he learned your name. I had prepared myself for this reality. I gave myself a pep talk about how he probably wouldn't know who I was. When I finally made my way to him, he looked at me and he paused. We made eye contact, his face became calm, and he just said, "It's you!" I knew that he didn't know my name but I also knew that he knew me. He had not forgotten.

So there I was, spending some time with this very special person when my aunt pulled me aside.

While she had been going through items in my grandparent's apartment, she had come across a random binder. She handed the binder over to me because she said she felt like it belonged to me.

I peeked inside and my world paused.

Inside this binder was every single thing I had ever written to Grandpa. Every poem, every horrible rhyme, every weird and ridiculous story, every card I had mailed him, every handwritten letter, every email. Every piece of writing that I had ever created and shared with him was inside this binder. He had saved each one, preserved in page protectors.

Even after all of these years, all of this time when I had forgotten who I was, when my true self was holding on for dear life in the cave behind my heart, he remembered. He knew who I was.

Here I stood, thinking I was a mature adult who knew exactly who she was and what she was doing: a scientist, a teacher, a yogi, a mom, a compassionate friend. That's who I am. That's what I've spent decades creating and going to school for and forging as my identity.

But no. For Grandpa, I would always be the girl who wrote unbelievably amazing things. I was the person who was going to write a book one day, an incredible book about all of my experiences. He never stopped believing that. He never forgot.

Why is she telling us this, you may be wondering. Seems personal, why would she share this? Let's give her some space, she's obviously losing it.

Ha! That's the thing. That's the whole point. I'm not losing it. I'm regaining it.

I have spent the last two chapters admitting that mindfulness can be blech. Awful. Heavy. Difficult. All of that is true and I meant every word. But why would I write an entire book about something that is terrible? Well, I wouldn't.

It is possible for mindfulness to feel heavy at times, but the truth is that, on a larger scale, in the big picture, at the end of the day, mindfulness is the answer. (Life Lesson #4) Mindfulness is where we press pause on the crazy train of our thoughts and take a time out. It's where we remember how to feel calm and then peaceful and then happy.

Mindfulness is how we remember.

Grandpa reminded me with that binder.

Everyone was right. That was the last time I saw him. He passed away less than a year after that visit. I was unable to attend his funeral. Four months later, I sat at a coffee shop with a friend who asked me, "What would you do with your life, if you could do anything?" I was stumped. I didn't know the answer.

Sitting in my bedroom later that day, I saw the binder sticking out of a messy stack of what I will call Stuff. Before mindfulness, I would have stuck this binder on the upper shelf of my bedroom closet, only to be discovered years later while deep cleaning (spoiler alert: I have never deep cleaned anything in my life). I wouldn't have thought about the binder for another moment.

As it was, I had spent the previous 8 years delving into mindfulness and sorting through my thoughts and feelings. I had a strong mindfulness practice and, because of this, I knew how to pause. In that pause, I pulled out the binder. I flipped through it and I could remember writing the awkward poems, the silly cards and letters. I saw what Grandpa saw: a curious girl with a twirly imagination and lots of quirky ideas.

The next day, I sat down and started writing the book that Grandpa always knew I would write.

Mindfulness brought me here. Ya, it sucked at first, but then it didn't. I stuck with it and one day I woke up to discover those superpowers that I had observed years before in a meditation professor at Cornell.

For, just as mindfulness makes us aware of the negative thoughts and emotions that we have been hiding from, it illuminates the positive as well. Just as my panic felt so huge that I could not contain it, I can now feel joy in that way. Joy so immense that my body cannot contain it and it leaks out of my eyes. Peace. Happiness. Gratitude. Connection. All of these are living within us. Sort through the negative, and these treasures come to light too.

Having a mental episode (breakdown, it was a breakdown). How unfortunate!

Discovering mindfulness. How fortunate!

Mindfulness really sucked. How unfortunate!

Mindfulness Superpowers. How fortunate!

Just as with the farmer and his wife, the story does not end here. There will be days when mindfulness does not feel good. There will be difficult events that happen in my life. The difference is that I no longer feel that they will crush me. I have the tools to work with anything that comes my way (except pink panties, never pink panties).

You can have this too.

How to Obtain Mindfulness Superpowers

Step 1. Get bitten by a mindfulness spider while on a field trip for school.

Eye roll. Noooo.

The first step is to obtain yoga leggings composed of vibranium.

<Sideways glance> Internal monologue: Are they buying it? Are they laughing or are they googling vibranium right now?

The concept of mindfulness is really easy to understand but can be difficult to carry out. All of us know this now. Obtaining mindfulness superpowers is exactly the same.

Let's turn once again to The Yoga Sutras, written looooong ago by Patanjali. It turns out lots and lots of people had trouble figuring out how to have a successful mindfulness practice.

According to Patanjali, your practice will be successful when it follows these three guidelines:

- You must do your practice for a long time (not days, weeks, or even months but more like years).
- Your practice must be consistent.
- You must be serious about your practice.

Duration. Consistency. Earnestness.

Duration

When I was taking my meditation course in college, I studied the topic for one semester, approximately 4 months. Then, I did not do any mindfulness for about 9 years. Patanjali says it is not enough to do mindfulness for just a little while. If you want to see results from your mindfulness practice, you must decide that you will practice it for a long time. Practicing for a few months and then never again will not provide any lasting benefits. The superpowers appear after you have been doing it for a long time.

There are research studies out there now that indicate your brain matter changes after just eight weeks of mindfulness practice. Isn't this interesting! Practicing mindfulness for any length of time is wonderful and fantastic and highly recommended. It can help you to get through difficult times. What Patanjali is saying is geared towards those superpowers. If you want consistent calm and awareness in your life, this will take a longer commitment to mindfulness.

Consistency

This is a tricky one. To be consistent in something means that you do it in the same way or stick with the same guidelines. After I came back to mindfulness, 9 years after my college class, I was inconsistent. I really needed some calm and peace in my life. I really wanted to use mindfulness. I had the best intentions. But I was inconsistent.

I would practice mindfulness for a few days and then would forget for another week. Then the stress levels would grow and I would come back to it for another day or so before falling away from it again. I continued in this way, practicing mindfulness for a week or so and then stopping for weeks and months at a time, for another 6 years.

While I was doing mindfulness, I noticed the effects. It did make me feel better. Life went smoother but I did not stick with it. Every time I fell away from mindfulness, the benefits immediately fell away too. I experienced the benefits but no superpowers.

Earnestness

To be earnest means to take something seriously. When we practice mindfulness in earnest, it means that we try our best. We take the task seriously. For example, when I go shopping for boots, I shop in earnest. I look at the boots from all angles; I compare prices; I ascertain the highest quality that I can afford. I am earnest about my boots.

When I was in my meditation class, I did indeed practice in earnest. I was living in horrible conditions, in terms of mindfulness, but those were my conditions at the time. I practiced when my roommate was out of the room and when most students were in class. I tried very hard to focus on what I was doing. I was trying my best with the conditions that I had.

Practicing in earnest does not mean practicing perfectly. It means trying your best to be mindful, regardless of the conditions that you find yourself in. It means trying to find suitable timing and conditions and then giving it your full attention, no matter what. It means being serious about the task, but walking away if it's not a productive session. Earnest. Not Perfect.

Mindfulness Practice = duration + consistency + earnestness

Make It Happen, People

Mindfulness superpowers are awesome. I am really just at the beginning of mine. I'm like a mindfulness sidekick. I have some superpowers but they aren't as powerful as they will be in another decade, when I will turn into my very own Mindfulness Superhero.

I am still in process. I am still learning. I am still practicing.

Following Patanjali's framework of duration, consistency, and earnestness was the magic recipe that made a difference. You can't just jump into his recipe though. (Well maybe you can, but most of us can't.) It takes some forethought and planning. You have to really want to do it.

What you are doing, essentially, is creating a new habit. A habit is a practice that you do regularly. That's exactly what we are trying to do, right?!

I brush my teeth every morning after breakfast and every night before bed. I bet you do something like this too. I don't even think about it. I don't eat breakfast and then say to myself, "Well, I guess you should go brush your teeth now." There is no thinking. I just do it. This is a habit.

Remember how every thought we have is a unique combination of neural pathways? And the pathways we travel more often become unconscious? We think the thoughts even without knowing we are thinking the thoughts? Yup. Same thing.

Every action or behavior we have is a unique combination of neural pathways. When you try to start a new behavior, it feels really hard. We are off-roading in the forest of our neurons. We are trying to combine different neurons. That's why it is so hard to create a new habit.

Now, brushing my teeth? Do you know how many years I have been brushing my teeth immediately after breakfast and then right before bed? So many years. Those neural pathways are deep, well-maintained paths in my neural forest. I don't even have to think about it. I eat breakfast and, without effort, I brush my teeth.

That is the type of habit we want to create with mindfulness.

There is a gigantic amount of research on the topic of habits. How to create them. How to stick with them. What to do when they aren't working. So many books, articles, TED Talks. What I have learned about habits has come from James Clear, both his TED Talk and his book.

Here's what I know. Two things:

Start small.

Attach mindfulness to a habit that you already have.

Start Small

One thing I have seen often while trying to teach mindfulness to adults is that they start too big. Their goal is grandiose. Maybe their goal is just medium-sized. Possibly their goal is very reasonable. Too big. All of that is too big.

Do not tell yourself that you will practice mindfulness for 20 minutes every day. 20 minutes?! Come on now. Don't even say 10 minutes. Do you know how long 10 minutes lasts when you are being mindful? It's forever. 5 minutes? Nope. Very reasonable but still too big.

How about 30 seconds.

Hear me out. Sounds too small, right? That won't make a difference at all, you're saying. Maybe, maybe not. When you are creating a habit, you aren't trying to make a difference. You are just trying to get the behavior ingrained in your neural network. You are forging a new path.

The best way to ensure that you stick with a behavior long enough to create a habit is to make it ridiculously, supremely easy.

I will practice mindfulness for 30 seconds every day.

Sure. Why not? Why wouldn't I stick with that? It's so easy.

Now, if you are practicing mindfulness and the 30 second timer goes off and you feel like doing a bit more, awesome. Bonus. It's all good. You're not saying you can't do mindfulness for longer. What you are saying is that you will do it for at least 30 seconds. Even on a terrible, rotten, end-of-the-world kind of day, you can do mindfulness for 30 seconds.

As you stick with this behavior over days/weeks, 30 seconds will start to feel way too easy and you will naturally start doing it for longer durations. You are growing the habit naturally instead of forcing the habit.

Attach Your Habit

The second secret to creating a new habit is to attach it to a habit that you already have. Instead of creating a brand new time or place to forge a habit, just link it up with an already successful one. Remember how you brush your teeth every day without even thinking about it? What if you decided to practice mindfulness for 30 seconds every day after you brush your teeth?

Your chances of remembering and sticking to a new behavior skyrocket when you attach it to something that you are already doing. The neural network is already in place. Instead of forging an entirely new path in the forest, you are traveling on an existing path and then just adding a tiny bit of new path at the end.

Here are some ways you can attach mindfulness to your day:

- After I wake up in the morning, I will get out of bed and do 30 seconds of mindfulness.
- After I brush my teeth at night, I will do 30 seconds of mindfulness.
- After I get home from school and throw my backpack recklessly down the hallway, I will do 30 seconds of mindfulness.
- After I do my daily chore of <insert chore here>, I will do 30 seconds of mindfulness.

To sum up, if you are interested in achieving mindfulness superpowers, your task looks something like this:

(duration + consistency + earnestness) + (start small + attach to a habit)

A math-y mindfulness equation. Laurent Schwartz would be proud.

~~LIFE LESSON #12: Must find vibranium.~~
For the record, I am up for that adventure.
LIFE LESSON #12: Superpowers = Duration + Consistency + Earnestness

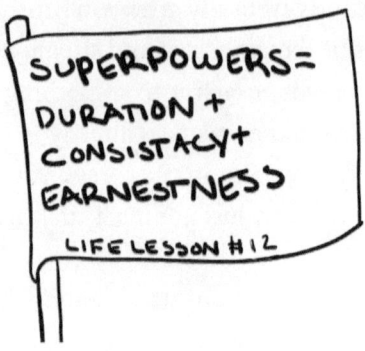

And one more. The very last life lesson for me to share!
~~LIFE LESSON #13: You would make an awesome superhero.~~
I really mean that, too.
LIFE LESSON #13: Sweetness awaits.

Chapter Summary

- Mindfulness Superpowers (calm, peace, awareness) can be obtained by maintaining a mindfulness practice that occurs over a long period of time, is consistent, and is done seriously.
- Duration: A mindfulness practice must be done over a long period of time if it will lead to superpowers. You must commit to practicing mindfulness for years. (Practicing for days, weeks, and months will still help you to feel good and can help you travel through life events. It just won't lead to superpowers.)
- Consistency: A mindfulness practice must be consistent. You must do it as a habit that you stick to over time. Practicing for a few weeks and then stopping for a few months and then coming back to it for a day or two can help you to feel calm in the moment but will not lead to lasting superpowers.
- Earnestness: A mindfulness practice must be approached seriously. You must try your best in the conditions that are present. You do not have to be perfect but you must attempt your highest effort. (This includes walking away when needed.)
- To create a lasting mindfulness habit, start small and attach mindfulness to a habit you already have.

To Do List

- Let's create your new mindfulness habit!
  - Choose the habit you already have.
  - Attach mindfulness to it. (What is your mindfulness goal? 30 seconds? 1 minute?)
  - Write it out in a statement: "After I _____ , I will practice mindfulness for _____."

- Celebrate! Every time you do your new habit, reinforce those neural networks by celebrating. Ideas:
  - High five yourself. (This is actually way fun.)
  - Jump up and down 3 times and declare your awesomeness.
  - Create a personal dance move. (You know which one.)
  - Eat a piece of chocolate. (Highly recommend)

Conclusion
The story goes like this...

Once upon a time, the little girl knew exactly who she was. She was curious and joyful. She liked the symmetry of flowers, the way dew droplets looked on blades of grass, and picking raspberries and apples in her grandparents' backyard.

Then... fortunately or unfortunately, life happened. She wore pink panties to school. Classmates laughed at her. Some called her names. She understood the emotions of shame and fear. Fortunately or unfortunately, she slowly learned to cover up her true self. She learned that it was not ok or acceptable or safe to be weird and silly. So she built layers.

She started to hide from the things she loved. She forgot how to look at flowers and how to crouch down to see the dew droplets. She grasped at things that felt happy and avoided things that made her feel badly about herself. Shame and fear felt so terrible so, fortunately or unfortunately, she pushed those emotions aside. She became a machine version of herself. This went on for so long that she started to think this robot-self was who she actually was.

She forgot who she really was.

Her true self grew to be very small, the size of her thumbnail. Fortunately or unfortunately, it retreated to the cave behind her heart, a safe hiding spot. There, it awaited the day when she would start to remember.

She pushed the uncomfortable emotions aside for years and years. Each time she did, they grew just a little bit larger. One day, they became as big as a white rhinoceros. With the strength of a white rhinoceros, the emotions exploded within her and she felt her world break into thousands of glittery pieces that rained down all around her like spiky dew droplets. She felt hopeless. She felt a lack of control. She felt strewn about as if she were trying to steer a sailboat through 15-foot seas.

When all of the pieces settled, she looked around. To her surprise, she noticed that her world was not what she had believed. The thoughts she had were inaccurate. The stories she had told herself were misleading and incorrect. Where she thought there were snakes, only coils of rope were present.

She paused. She breathed. She observed. As she looked around the rubble that had been her life, she spotted a flower. One flower.

Fortunately or unfortunately, she remembered.

She remembered dew droplets, and raspberries, and what it felt like to be curious and joyful.

And so she got to work.

She made a habit of pausing every day so that she could pull out of the thoughts and emotions. It was not always easy and it did not always feel good, but she persisted, as stubborn as a white rhinoceros. Instead of snakes, she started to find ropes. Instead of shame and fear, she found peace and acceptance.

Fortunately or unfortunately, she coexists with her true self to this very day, living happily ever after (more or less) and eating lots of chocolate.

And isn't that interesting.

A Mindful Compendium of Not Quite Life Lessons

Not Quite Life Lesson #1:
Never wear pink panties.

Not Quite Life Lesson #2:
Buy new boots.

Not Quite Life Lesson #3:
I must eat chocolate.

Not Quite Life Lesson #4:
Buy a new bike.

Not Quite Life Lesson #5:
The genie will destroy you.

Not Quite Life Lesson #6:
Horror movies are too scary.

Not Quite Life Lesson #7:
Fourthfoldly, Danielle makes up a lot of words.

Not Quite Life Lesson #8:
Whatever you do, don't think about spiders.

Not Quite Life Lesson #9:
Fish can't climb trees so let Einstein do it.

Not Quite Life Lesson #10:
Internships are so much fun.

Not Quite Life Lesson #11:
Danielle went an entire chapter without mentioning chocolate.

Not Quite Life Lesson #12:
Must find vibranium.

Not Quite Life Lesson #13:
You would make an awesome superhero.

A Mindful Compendium of Life Lessons

Life Lesson #1:
Sometimes, life sucks.

Life Lesson #2:
Well, isn't that interesting.

Life Lesson #3:
You are not your thoughts.

Life Lesson #4:
Mindfulness is the answer.

Life Lesson #5:
The present moment is where it's at.

Life Lesson #6:
Don't resist. Coexist. (with your thoughts, that is)

Life Lesson #7:
Learn mindfulness NOW, adolescents.

Life Lesson #8:
Sitting mindfulness = Sit + Focus + Refocus + Repeat

Life Lesson #9:
Anything can be mindfulness.

Life Lesson #10:
It's time to stop hiding.

Life Lesson #11:
Pay attention. (Is it a snake or a rope?)

Life Lesson #12:
Superpowers = duration + consistency + earnestness

Life Lesson #13:
Sweetness awaits.

Epilogue

I did buy those olive green boots. The soles are wooden clogs. They are glorious. In fact, every time I wear them, I am glorious. Unstoppable. Go ahead and try to stop me - I dare you.

After wearing them for the first time, I arrived home - feeling all incredible - and sat down to take them off. They do not have zippers. They are pull on boots. I sat down and yanked the boot, but it would not come off. Yanked harder. Wow, my foot did not want to let go.

On a final, super strength pull, the boot flew off my foot and the wooden clog sole hit me right between the eyes.

My eyes immediately teared up. My family immediately laughed at me.

I walked around with a big, bruised lump between my eyes for a week or so.

Two things:

1. They are still my favorite boots ever. I wear them every chance I get but everyone keeps their distance when it's time to take them off.
2. They are the last pair of boots I have purchased.

And that's all I have to say about that.

Acknowledgments

To Bree - Good morning. I see the assassins have failed.

To Katy - We are both Most Excellent.

To Jess - Three words: adventure, curiosity, friendship

To Susan - Mahna mahna

To Kevin - For sitting with me at coffee one morning and starting this whole process.

To Evey, my scary adolescent daughter - Thank you for not rolling your eyes when you read this book. Your non-eye roll meant the world to me.

To Liam, my less scary adolescent son - You would never roll your eyes at me. That's why you're my favorite son.

To Earl - Who doesn't mind how weird I am. There's no one in the world who doesn't mind more than you.

To the family I've created along the way and without whom I would certainly be a different, less amazing person: Allison Fluffypants, Amy, Anna Leigh, Chrys, CU Ohana, De, Debbie, Heather, Heidi, Julie, Kat, Kisha, Krista, Lyn, Mamie, Marion, Meredith, Moore, Peggy, Sonia, Ursel.

Danielle Parker accepted her first job working with adolescents a zillion years ago in 2003. Ever since then, she has worked with this age group as often as possible in a variety of jobs, from classroom teacher to guides at nature centers, animal shelters, and even the health department. She finds them quirky, honest, and hilarious. (Translation: She thinks you're weird.) She has a B.S. in biology from Cornell University, an M.A.T. from East Carolina University, and an M.S. in coastal zone management from Nova Southeastern University. She completed her Secondary Montessori training in 2021 through Houston Montessori Center. She is a 500-RYT yoga instructor and is dedicated to her personal mindfulness journey. For the record, pink has always been and is still to this day Danielle's least favorite color.